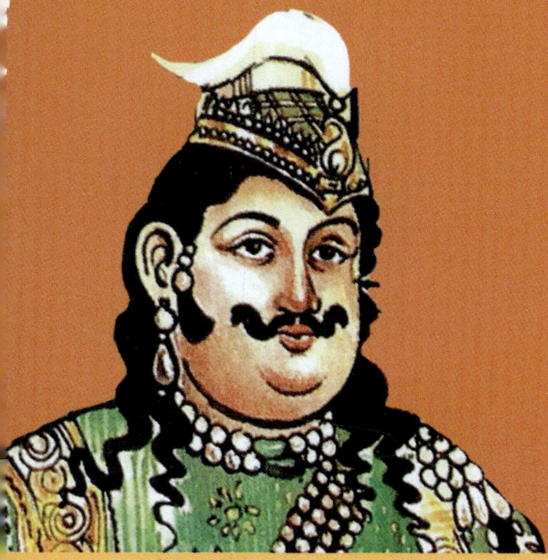

# Love Songs of Nawab Wajid Ali Shah

## नवाब वाजिद अली शाह के श्रृंगार पद

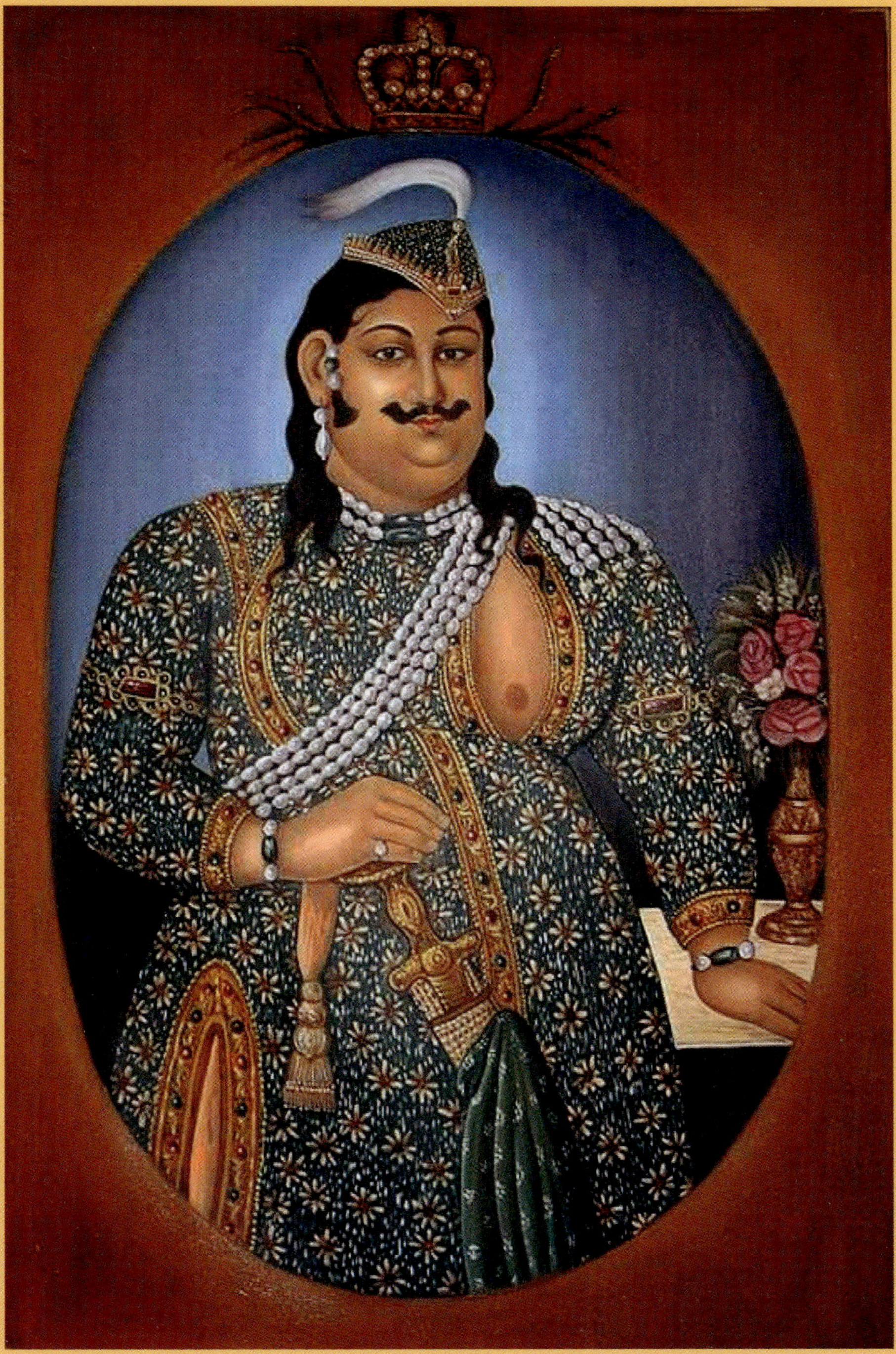

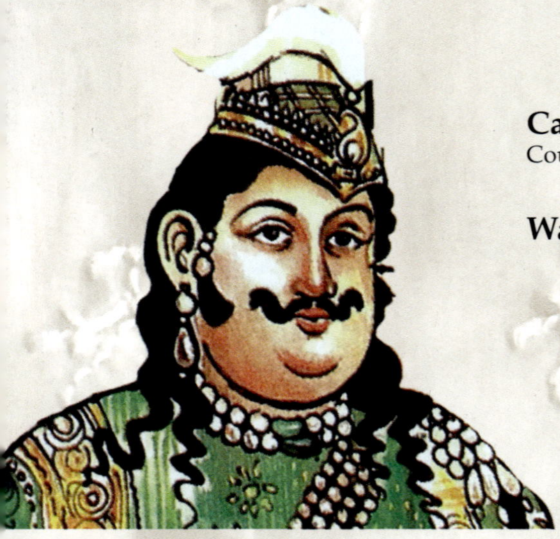

**Cataloging in Publication Data--DK**
Courtesy: D.K. Agencies (P) Ltd. <docinfo@dkagencies.com>

**Wajid 'Ali Shah,** *King of Oudh,* 1822-1887, **author.**
Love songs of Nawab Wajid Ali Shah = Navāba Vājida Alī Śāha ke śr̥ṅgāra pada / Muzaffar Ali [and six others] ; paintings, Padma Shri Vijay Sharma & associates.
pages cm
English, Hindi and Awadhi.
Includes bibliographical references.
ISBN 9788124610664 (softbound)

1. Wajid 'Ali Shah, King of Oudh, 1822-1887 — Translations into Hindi. 2. Wajid 'Ali Shah, King of Oudh, 1822-1887 — Translations into English. 3. Love poetry. 4. Love in art. 5. Miniature painting, Indic. 6. Awadhi poetry. 7. Awadhi poetry — Translations into Hindi. 8. Awadhi poetry — Translations into English. I. Ali, Muzaffar, 1944- translator, editor. II. Sharma, Vijay, 1962- artist. III. Wajid 'Ali Shah, King of Oudh, 1822-1887. Songs. Selections. IV. Wajid 'Ali Shah, King of Oudh, 1822-1887. Songs. Selections. Hindi. V. Wajid 'Ali Shah, King of Oudh, 1822-1887. Songs. Selections. English. VI. Title. VII. Title: Navāba Vājida Alī Śāha ke śr̥ṅgāra pada.

LCC PK1947.9.W35A6 2020 | DDC 891.492 23

**ISBN: 978-81-246-1066-4**


**Paintings:** Padma Shri Vijay Sharma & Associates
**Layout:** Shrinidhi Sridhar, Ottawa, ON, Canada
**Photographer:** Sanjay Kumar, Lucknow

**Fonts**
ITC Garamond
Remachine Script
Sanskrit words are italicized



Printed and published by:
**D.K. Printworld (P) Ltd.**
"Vedasri", F-395, Sudarshan Park
New Delhi - 110015
Phs.: 011-25453975, 25466019
e-mail: indology@dkprintworld.com
web: www.dkprintworld.com

# Contents

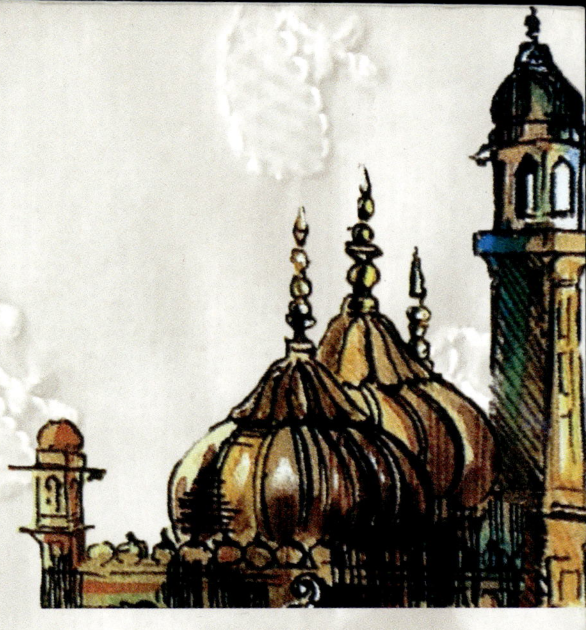



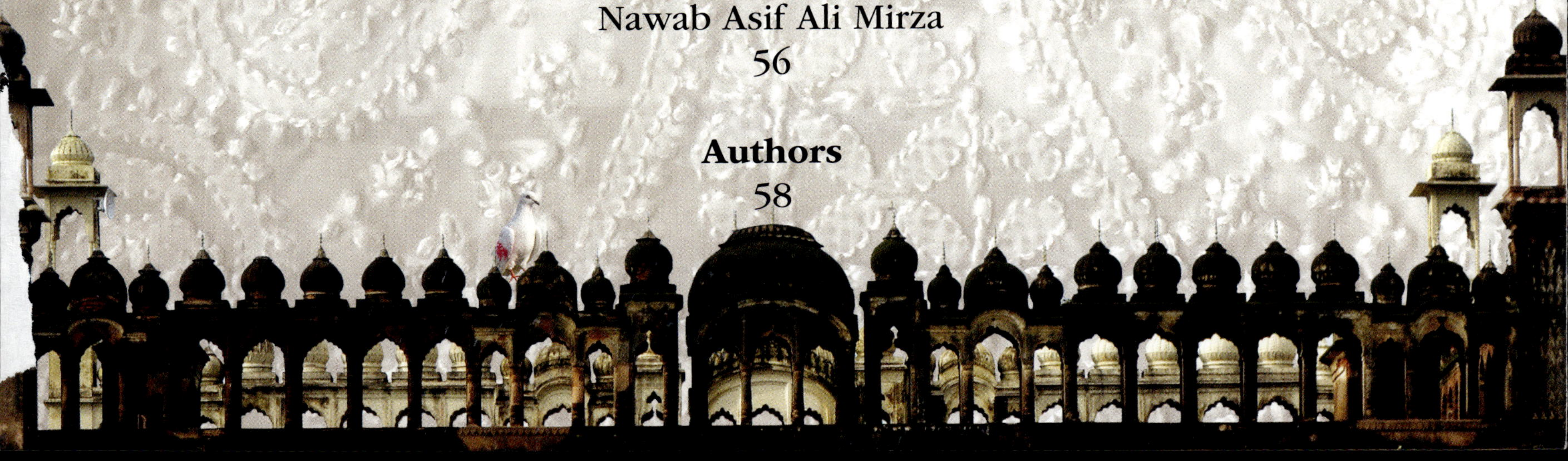

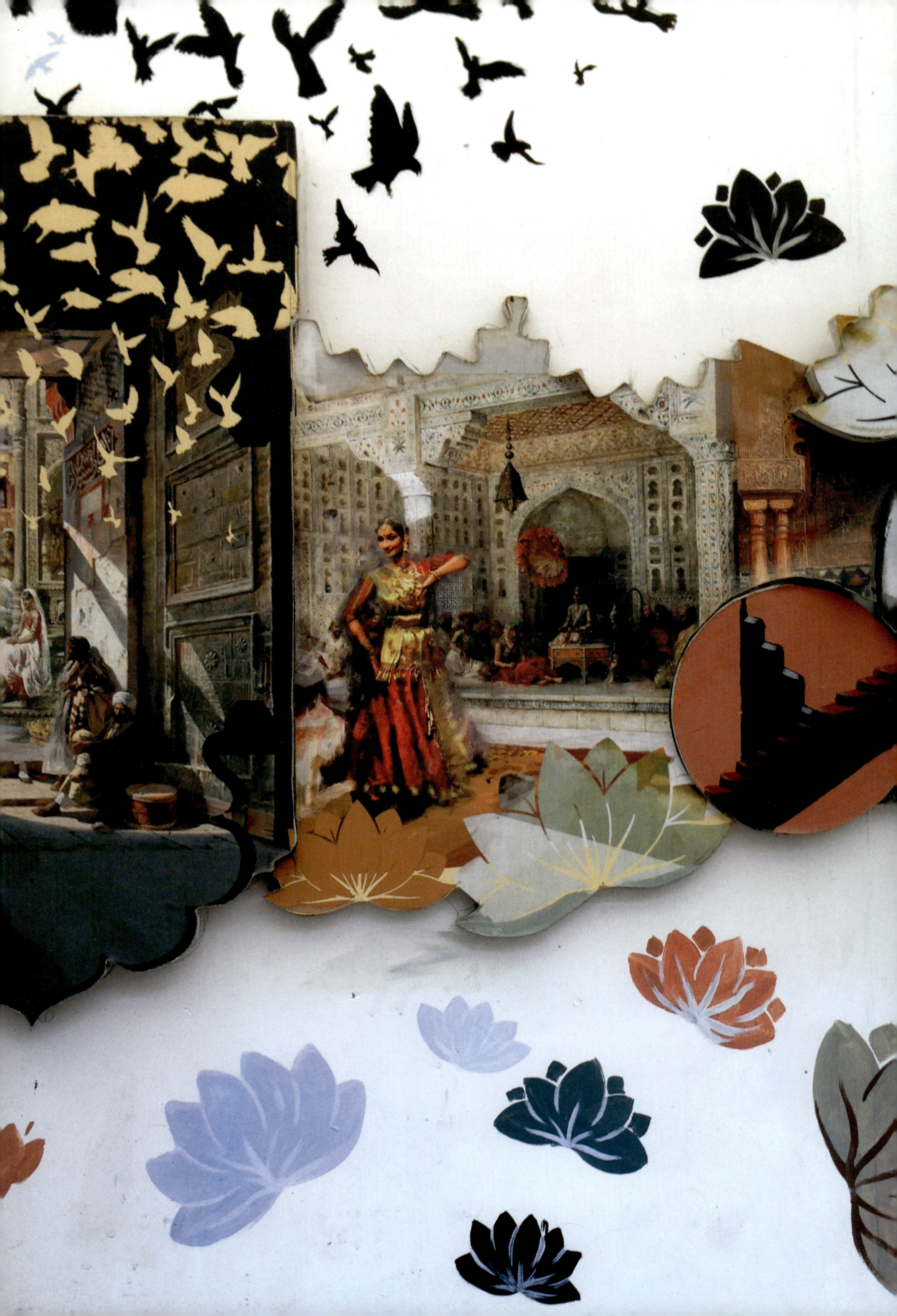

# Dedication

Even today on a moonlit night
when one walks the bylanes and pathways of Lucknow
one still hears the hushed sounds of Kathak dancers
the whispers of musicians, the tinkling of *ghungroo*s.
One has visions of the shimmer of silk and the beauty of *chickankari*
in lush environments of palaces and *haveli*s, mansions and ateliers.
Where, when the wind blows through the trees, one hears
*ghazal*s and *thumri*s of the love of Radha and Krishna.
Where the Ganga–Jamuni *tehzeeb* is how we live with each other
through the commerce of the day and the charm of romantic nights.
And narrow lanes still have the aroma of Awadhi cuisine
where life was lived to its fullest and the senses totally saturated.
Where people pursued a life of pleasure even as they
celebrated a culture of music and dance, song and poetry.
And then suddenly from the heavens above
as strains of *babul mora* were heard
one saw the *nawab* who made all this possible
and we offered our salutations to a person
for whom to live was to love
and to love was to surely know.

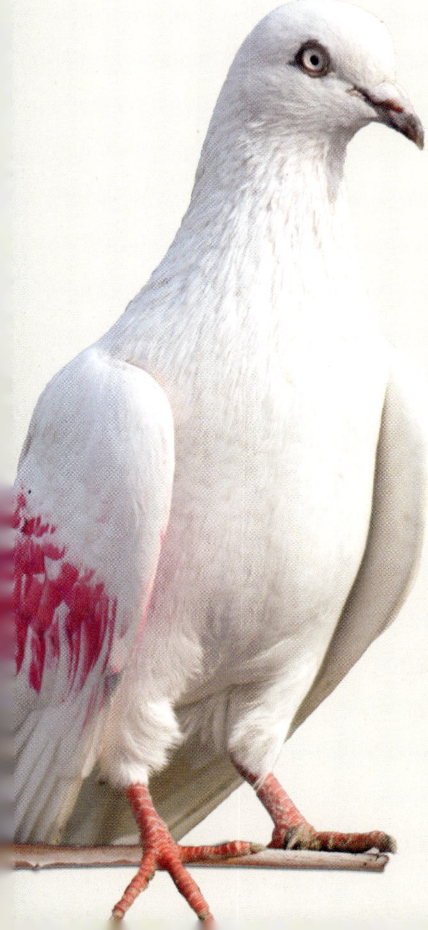

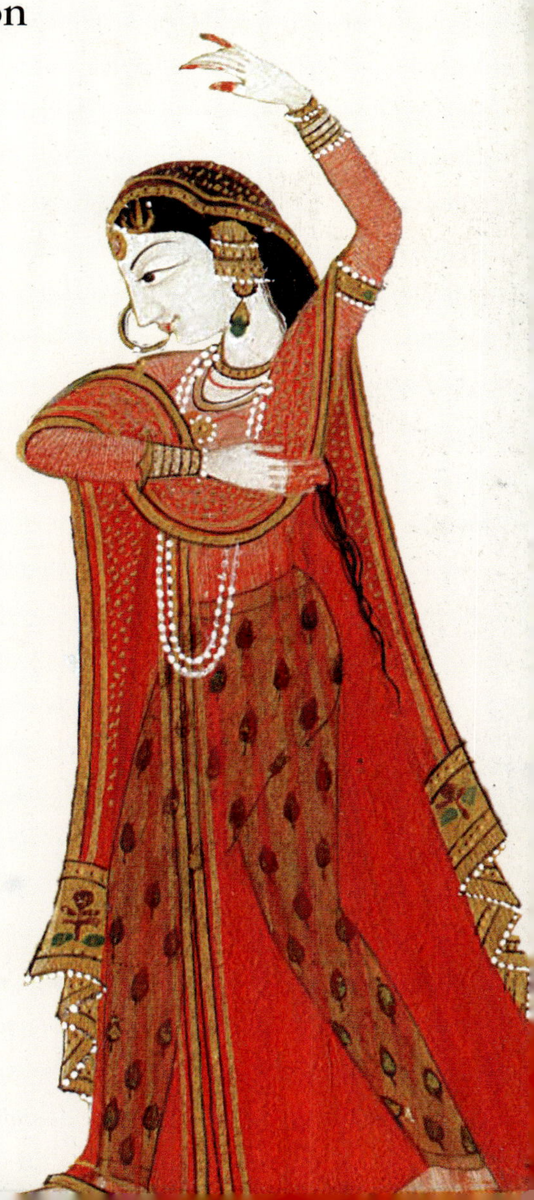

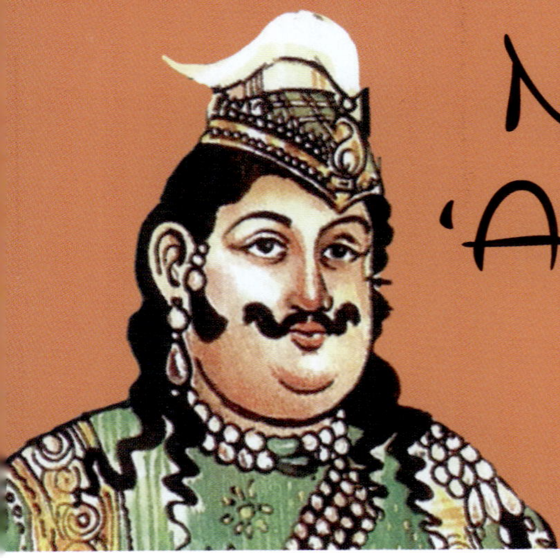

# Haye Lucknow: Nawab Wajid Ali Shah 'Akhtar' – A Poet's Profile

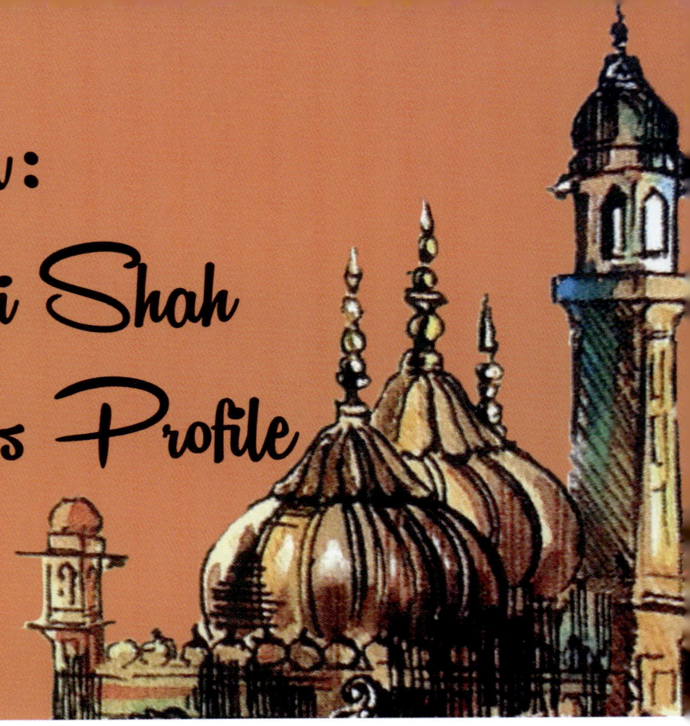

**Muzaffar Ali**

*har-chand laakh tarah bhulātā huuñ yaad ko*
*'akhtar' pukār uthā hai dil haye lakhnau*

Each moment, in a thousand ways,
to wipe my memories off,
I tried, yet each instant this helpless
heart of Akhtar cried,
Oh my Lucknow!

The important fact is that Wajid Ali Shah is relevant today because he left behind a legacy of love. A legacy which we still cherish. A legacy we live and breathe. He left behind a city as a beloved, as abstract and as ethereal as a piece of paradise, for us to dream about. A garden of his dreams, he lovingly crafted and called Qaiserbagh, remembered till this day as a garden of the soul! In its fold, it held close to its heart – music, poetry and dance. A garden where the shadow of Krishna lurked in each *jharokha* and the *payal* of each *gopi* glistened and echoed from the dew on the blades of its grass. He made it a poet's dream and asked the poet Ameer Meenai to wander through its gardens for poetic inspiration. And when he departed surrendering his heart to the tyranny of the usurpers he left Qaiserbagh in the care of the morning breeze. It was none other than Wajid Ali Shah who could create an ambience of poetry for poets. A heart that was prepared to face a world of turmoil and the agony of separation from the beloved. He had seen the best and the worst. Lived on hope. Faced despair. Dreamt of better days which gently averted him in his time in exile in Matia Burj in Calcutta.

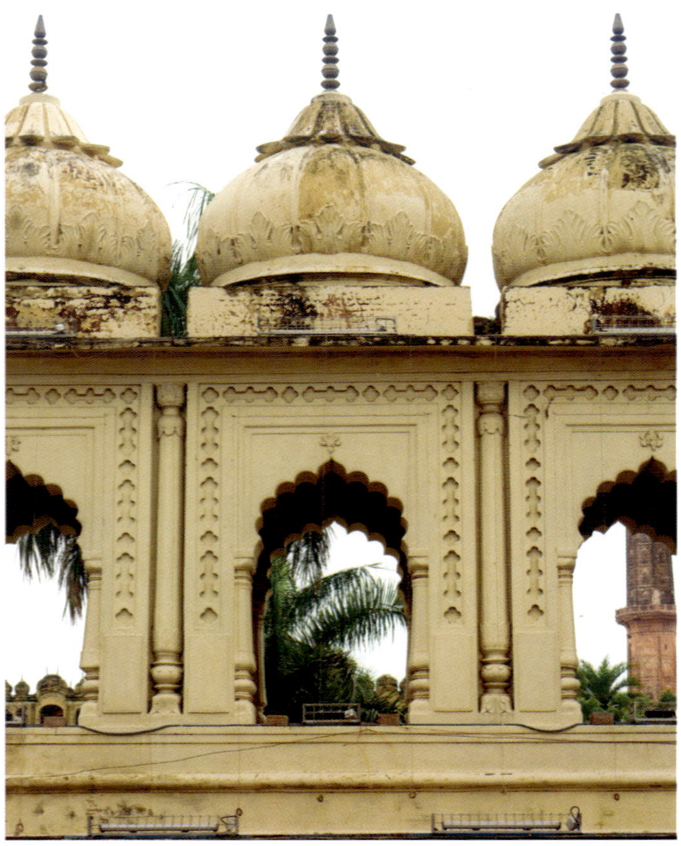

*Lakhi Gate*

He saw poetry in the elegies of Karbala. In the martyrdom of Imam Husain. The three days of thirst of the infant Asghar. The chivalry of Abbas … in which he saw love, faith, valour and sacrifice. He saw poetry in the forlorn love of Radha for Krishna, where the poet is privy to the language of the peacock and the deer, the birds and the swans, the leopards and the tigers. He loved them all.

It was difficult to be born with an open vulnerable heart and become a victim of a larger colonial design to usurp his beauteous garden of Awadh.

*ya mujhe afsar e*
*shahana na banaya hota*
*ya mera taj gadaya*
*na banaya hota …*

It was this tone found in the poetry of Bahadur Shah Zafar that resonated in the poetry of Wajid Ali Shah or possibly every ruler of that tumultuous time who had a mind and heart of his own and a sense of dignity and independence.

The poetry of Krishna prepared Akhtar for his long exile in Matia Burj. He pined for his people and the people pined for him creating an ongoing bridge of poetry. The illusion of the Beloved adorned his poetry and embellished his music. He wrote in music fusing his pain into the *raga*s. The throbbing of the restless heart became his *gat*s and his *toda*s. The canvas of his creativity engulfed a world full of artistes marooned in his universe of love and despair in the refuge of Matia Burj. An ironic name for his final milestone. Sometimes it is difficult to fathom what he went through, what came out and what remained buried deep within. But as imagination bloomed with inspiration of Wajid Ali Shah so many new unseen dimensions seemed to emerge.

In the eyes of some he may not be a great master but he was beyond all that masters are made up of. An enigma of a romance that ever lived and was shattered over and over again! His poetry was oozing with a romance that even a simple utterance in rhyme became more impactful, more painful, more passionate when heard in retrospect in the backdrop of his predicament. They became the

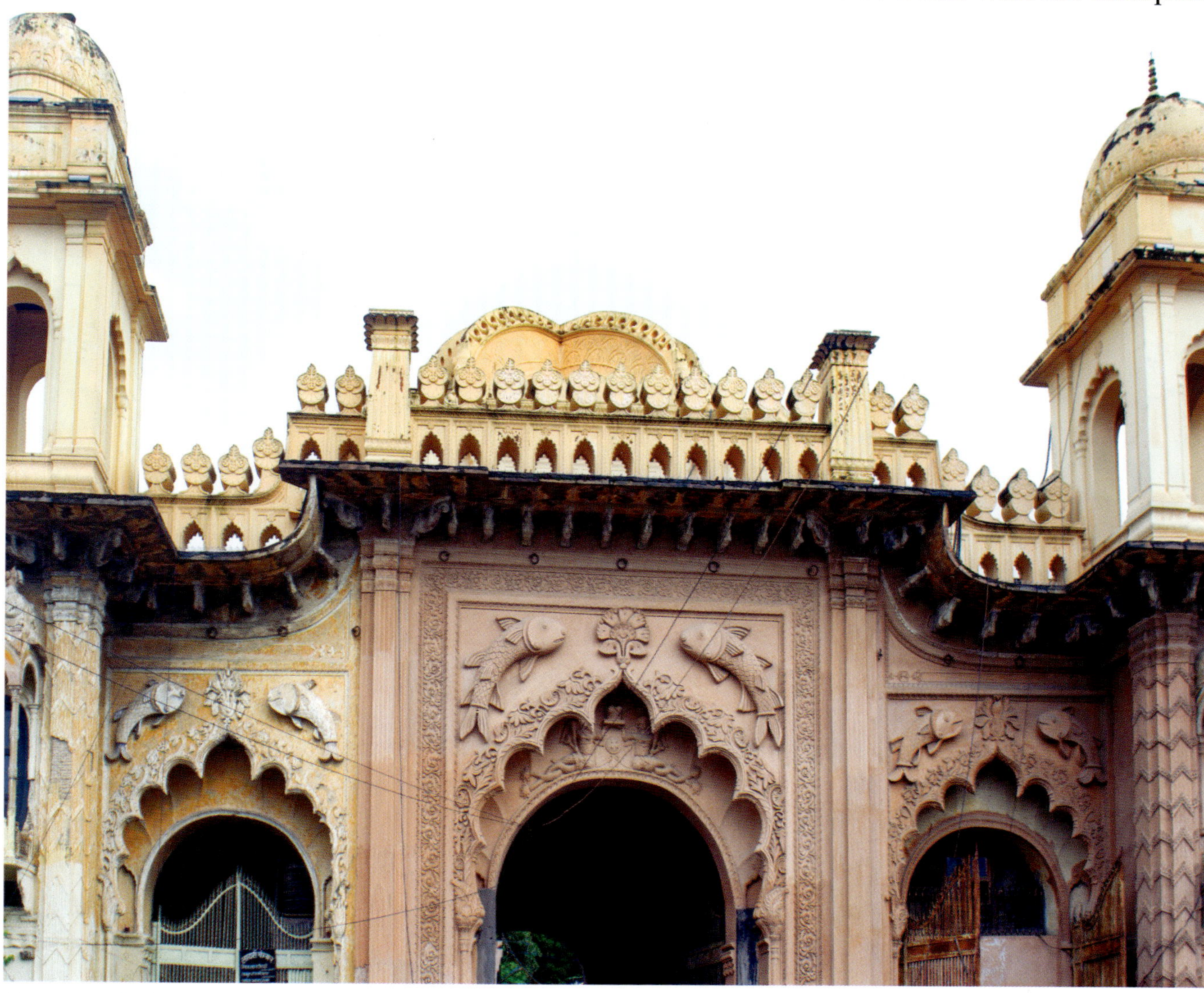

*Canopy over Bada Imambara*

*thumris* of the soul that live on in time.

*Babul mora naihar chhooto jai*. It compared with *kahe ko biyahe bides* of Hazrat Amir Khusrau, with whom we discover he had much in common.

*gori soye sej pe mukh pe daale kes,*
*chal khusrau ghar aapne saanjh bhayi chaudes*

His seminal verse was on the leaving of his beloved city and his abode in Qaiserbagh that he had so lovingly built.

*dar o divar pe hasrat se nazar karte hain*
*khush raho ahle chaman ham to safar karte hain*
*hamne apne dil e nazuk ko jafa ko saunpa*
*qaiseri bagh jo hai usko saba ko saunpa*
*dar o deevar pe hasrat se nazar karte hain*
*khush raho ahle watan ham to safar karte hain ...*

He was the most tender-hearted soul that Mother India bore on her soil and would be proud to boast of. And much to the disappointment of his oppressors, it was his tragic life that allowed this to happen and made him truly immortal as an artiste who followed his heart. It was the trajectory of this angst which gave him a vast vocabulary of feelings to understand poetry, find music in poetry and poetry in music till it became dance and a dance that was sacred.

As a Shia he was at home with the metaphor of pain and human sacrifice for the love of God and Truth as experienced in the martyrdom of Imam Husain. He knew the meaning of thirst; what a river of tears meant; the suffering of a broken heart and finally the union with the Maker. He knew how important it was to share this feeling with mankind so that such suffering would not happen on the face of our world again. He expressed all this through poetry, flowing like the river of life. He wrote less but felt what he wrote. He lived in an ambience of poetry where it was equally important to listen to heartbeats around him, than to immerse himself in his own feelings. What he felt about Lucknow, Lucknow feels about him. ....

When he left, when he lived in hope and till now over a century after he has departed. ...

*allāh ai buto hamein dikhlāye lakhnau*
*sote meñ bhī ye kahte haiñ ham haye lakhnau*
Oh Allah! Oh my beloveds! show me my Lucknow
For as I sleep I am known to say Oh my Lucknow!

*aisā huā huuñ hijr meñ us ke nahīf-o-zār*
*dekhe agar mujhe vahīñ sharmāye lakhnau*
Oh my beloved! ask me not of my state being away from thee. ...
For if you did it will shame you no end, Oh my Lucknow!

*aaye na mere paas to maiñ aap hī chalūñ*
*mujh ko ḳhudā kare kahīñ bulvāye lakhnau*

If my beloved does not come to me
then I will go to her
I wish to God I'm beckoned soon
by my Lucknow.

*gulshan ajab bahār ke har qasr rashk-e-ḳhuld*
*aur gomtī ġhazab kī hai dariyā-e-lakhnau*

Beds of flowers in unusual bloom, gardens rival paradise
And of Gomti do not ask my friends, the river of my love, my Lucknow.

*hūr-o-paī ko rashk thā ik ek shaḳhs par*
*be-misl thhe sabhī mah-e-sīmā-e-lakhnau*

Even fairies envied each beauty here
Unrivalled were these beauties of my beauty, my Lucknow.

*marne ke baad bhi na mitegā jigar se daagh*
*jannat meñ ham ko hoyegī parvā-e-lakhnau*

Even after I depart
these scars from the soul will not leave
Even in paradise I'll sit and
think of my beauty, my Lucknow.

*maiñ kyā kahūñ faqīroñ ko jo kuchh ġhurūr thā*
*ik ik gadā-e-shahr thā dārā-e-lakhnau*

What say of the dignity of the *faqir*s of the city
Every humble dispossessed
was a Sultan in my Lucknow.

It was the love of his Lucknow that made him truly a *fakir* who saw divinity in its absence. He began to prefer the humble headgear of a *fakir* to the worldly crown of a king. He saw the path of the divine tavern beyond all heavens.

*dastār-e-faqīrāna ik taaj se afzūñ hai*
*rāh-e-tarah-e-khum-ḳhāna merāj se afzūñ hai*

The turban of a *fakir*
is beyond the crown of the king
The path to the tavern beyond the way to heaven.

*aise hī hukūmat hai aise hī ibādat hai*
*ye shāh-e-faqīrāna mohtāj se afzūñ hai*
This is the way to rule and this is the way to pray
This kingly *faqir* is beyond the king who is a *fakir*.

*chalte ho paristāñ meñ pariyāñ haiñ bahut shāyeq*
*ab husn-e-parī-ḳhāna phir aaj se afzūñ*
Come to the land of fairies, where the fairies wait for thee
The beauty of this fairyland from now is beyond what it has ever been.

*phir hoye fuzūñ daulat 'aḳhtar' ye duā de tū*
*ye faqra-e-pīrāna ik raaj se afzūñ hai*

Let the wealth of the world go where it belongs
Oh Akhtar! bless this realm of saints that is beyond kingship of the kings. ...

He bore with fortitude the embarrassment he was made to face as a ruler. And he expressed this in words that are etched on our hearts!

*sahe ġham paye raftagāñ kaise kaise*
*mire kho gaye kārvāñ kaise kaise*

What shall I say
How I bore my grief
Without friends and companions,
my caravan lost
No follower seems to be around
No one to share love's tale in brief. ...

*vo chitvan vo̊ abrū vo qad yaad sab hai*
*sunāoñ maiñ guzre bayāñ kaise kaise*

Her wild stance, her arched eyebrow, her statuesque grace, I remember all,
Images gone by, with pain I recall.

*rahā ishq se naam majnūñ kā varna*
*tah-e-ḳhāk haiñ be-nishāñ kaise kaise*
Majnun amidst lovers, is on the highest rung. ...
Yet many nameless ones haven gone into the earth unheard unsung.

*shab-e-vasl meiñ mah ko uryāñ kareñge*
*ayaañ hoñge rāz-e-nihāñ kaise kaise*
In the night of our union we will unveil the moon
The secrets within will unfold soon.

Nawab Wajid Ali Shah is an enigma and an open secret. He is as much hidden as he is revealed.

It is time that we celebrate all that he stood for. From inner freedom to outer captivity. A philosopher, a Sufi and a Sultan and above all a Human.

*bahr-e-lam meiñ ye insaan haiñ mānind-e-habab*
*dam meñ bante haiñ ye dam-bhar meñ fan hote haiñ*

The human being is but a bubble
in the ocean of existence
Born in an instant and gone in the next. ....

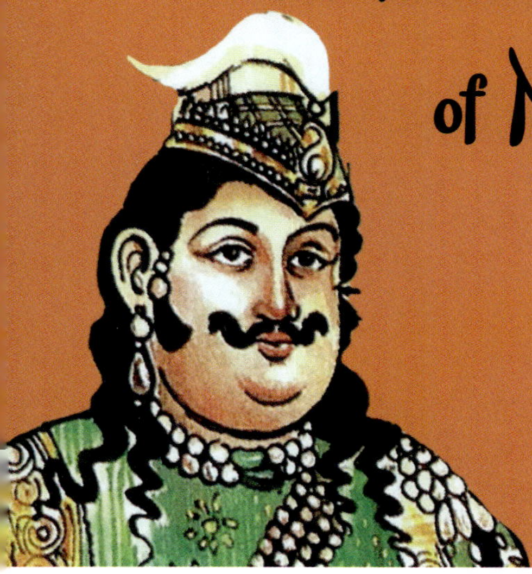

# Music and Dance During the Period of Nawab Wajid Ali Shah

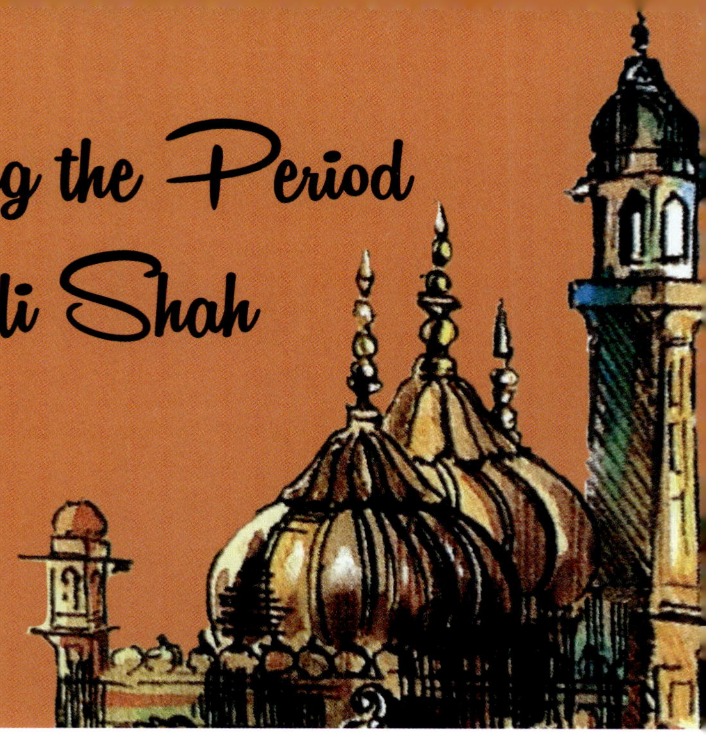

**Shovana Narayan**

In the nineteenth century, Lucknow and Nawab Wajid Ali Shah were synonymous with culture and cuisine, music and dance. As far back as in 1874, a New York-based journalist visited Lucknow to see for himself the great wealth and grandeur of this Lucknow Nawab Wajid Ali Shah and his decline into penury in Matia Burj where he spent his last days. The style in which he lived even after his ouster gave a glimpse into what would have been the cultural life of Awadh at Lucknow in its heyday.

Muhammad Faiz-Baksh, in *Tarikh-i-Farahbaksh* observed that:

> No ruler of any country lived in such refinement, and pomp … as Nawab Shuja-ud Daulah, and also it seemed that … all sorts of expert artistes, craftsmen and students from every direction … made Faizabad their domicile.

However, what led to Awadh becoming a cultural hub that attracted artistes from all over, is a story by itself. It was Asaf ud-Daulah who shifted the capital of Awadh in 1775 from Faizabad to Lucknow. He soon made Lucknow a cultural hub with fine buildings like the Imambara, Rumi Darwaza and many others in a bid to rival the splendour of Faizabad. Awadh's prosperity and richness together with the interest of the Nawabs also created a favourable environment for patronage of various aspects of culture, architecture, cuisines, sports such as kite flying and cock fights, Urdu *shayari*, *thumri* music, *dastangoi,* dance and dance-dramas. Various texts such as those of Syed Masood Hasan Rizvi Adeeb, author and scholar of Urdu literature, describe the *dastangoi* that had its roots in *Kissa Khawani* of Persia.

Historian Abdul Halim Sharar has commented upon the increasing importance of Lucknow in the eighteenth and nineteenth centuries which had been a sleepy town under the Mughals. But as the central authority of Delhi started declining after Aurangzeb, Gazi-ud-din Haider established the autonomy of Awadh that stretched from the Garhwal hills in the north-west to Bihar in the south-east. He also comments that the emerging Lucknow culture was, to a large extent, a derivative of the culture witnessed in Delhi. Hussain has quoted the Urdu poet, Insha who had migrated from Delhi to Lucknow:

> So many nobles forsook Delhi for Lucknow that Delhi became empty and Lucknow full. Of this multitude, there was none whose ancestry or residence had been in Lucknow for more than a century.

Thus Lucknow benefited from the declining power of Delhi. This resulted in the emergence of a new class of nouveau riche who tried to emulate the lifestyle of the cultured elite of Delhi. The result of their newly-acquired cultural sensibilities and a keen desire to have their presence was felt especially in the genres of music, dance and architecture.

The region of Awadh saw increased interaction between the Hindu and Muslim communities. In fact, right from the start, despite Muslim hegemony in the north of India, Hindu culture had always influenced art and culture. Brajbhasha was the dominant language of Lucknow while Urdu with Persian influence and Hindi with Sanskrit undertones were also popular. The difference between Mughal and Awadhi culture lies in the fact that the royal dialect of the courts of Awadh percolated to the streets and lanes to evolve and flourish among the common subjects in Lucknow, while Mughal courts restricted its language to the nobility and royalty. Educated Hindus of Lucknow mastered the art of Urdu and Persian. They even took to wearing *angarakha* and visited the Imambaras and *dargahs*. The Muslims including the Shia Awadh rulers such as Nawab Wajid Ali Shah, celebrated Hindu festivals too. During Nawab Wajid Ali Shah's time, the *rahas* dance-dramas based on Hindu deities, the Jogiya festivals and Hori celebrations were noteworthy. Many Muslim poets adopted Hindu pen-names and wrote hymns in praise of Hindu gods. This came to be known as the Ganga–Jamuni *tehzeeb* of Lucknow.

Lucknow had a wide range of performing artistes, from the sophisticated and the skilled to the common street performers. If there were the skilled Kathaks and the *bhagats* or the *raasleela* artistes who performed on special occasions, there were also the *dastangoi* performers, and the performances of the *natwas*, the *bhands*, the *nakkalis*, the common female performers such as the *jalsewalis*, the *chunewalis*, the *domnis* and the *natanis*, magicians, puppet shows by wandering gypsies who performed in fairs and gatherings for the common man. There were also various categories of musicians such as the *qawwals*, *beenkaars*, *rababiyas*, *sardiyas* and those who trained bears in dances namely the *reechhwale kalandars* and those who also trained monkeys and goats to perform.

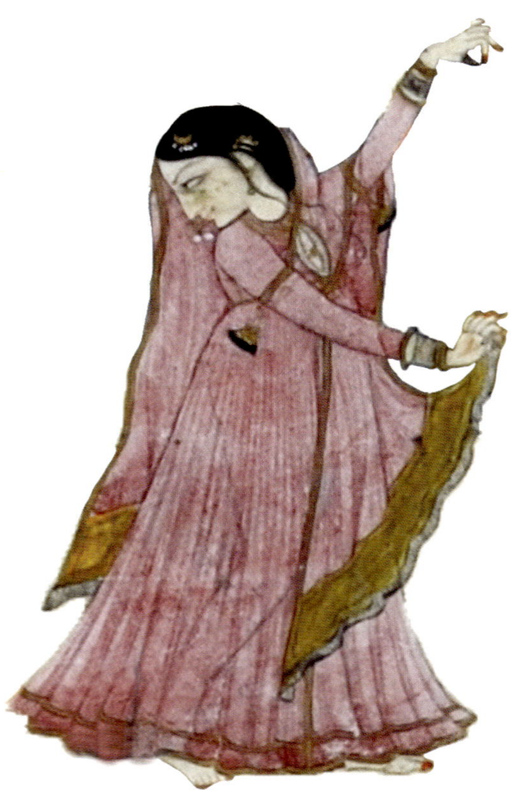

As per epigraphical and historical records available, the Brahmin Kathak performers that had dotted the religious and cultural scenario of India ever since the early Mauryan period, encountered resistance with the onset of Muslim rule in the medieval period of Indian history. Kathak, essentially a Hindu temple dance form, received patronage from some Muslim rulers in spite of their Islamic faith. Emperor Akbar's period saw one of the early successful attempts at harmonizing the seemingly two disparate approaches especially towards dance. Traditional Islam considered dance to be *haram* whereas traditional Hindu India considered it a path of religious devotion. Even though dance by only women was permitted in Islam on certain occasions or dance by some of the Sufi *dervishes*, yet any reference to God or his deeds through legends as done by the Kathaks was prohibited. Thus the Kathaks, by nature of their art form and by circumstances, were restricted to the temples in those times.

However, the court of Awadh stated a different story. Records speak of several Kathak stalwarts receiving patronage from the rulers of Awadh. During the *subedari* of Saadat Ali Khan II, Ghazi-ud-din Haider and Nasir-ud-din Haider, the prominent Kathak performers in their court were Ram Sahay, Beni Prasad, Dayalji and Hiralalji. Names of eminent Kathaks such as Khushi Maharaj at the time of Shuja ud-Daulah and Asaf ud-Daulah, Kathaks such as Halalji, Prakashji, Dayaluji during the reign of Nawab Sadat Ali Khan and Durga Prasadji and Thakur Prasadji in Nawab Wajid Ali Shah's reign, and thereafter Kalika Prasad and Bindadin Maharaj, have been recorded by Abdul Halim Sharar. From the records of this period, it appears that these Kathaks were not only great performers but were also regarded highly as teachers.

Besides the richness and favourable cultural ethos of Awadh, famines in the eastern part of Awadh State (and of present-day UP, Bihar and Bengal) led to migration of artistes to Lucknow and enriching it. It was such a famine coupled with personal tragedies that led the forefathers of Pandit Birju Maharaj to leave their ancestral home in Kichakila village in Handia Tehsil near Allahabad in the nineteenth century and seek better prospects in the court of Awadh. It goes to the credit of the Shia Nawabs of Awadh to accord patronage to the Hindu Brahmin Kathaks, which subsequently led to the establishment of the Lucknow *gharana* of Kathak. Till then, their performances were known as the Dance of the Kathak Log but from now onwards their dance form came to be known as Kathak, derived from the community that they belonged to.

It may not be out of place to mention the interrelationship and consequent dilemmas of the Hindu Kathaks vis-à-vis the Muslim courts that is best captured in the recorded anecdote by Priya Das in Bhaktamol of Nabhaji in 1772. Apparently, Narayan Das's fame as a Kathak had spread far and wide, causing the local Muslim ruler, the Mir, to request him to perform in his court. This request of the Mir filled Narayan Das with dismay because, used as he was to dancing before the idol of his *ishta-devata,* he however could not do so in the Mir's court. In case he refused, the consequences would have been severe. Finally, he found a solution to his dilemma and performed in the Mir's court before a *tulsi mala* symbolic of Krishna, instead of an idol. From now on this solution was universally followed by all other devout Kathaks who performed either before a *tulsi mala* or before a *rudraksh mala,* in case they were requested to perform in a Muslim court. Mutual respect was also the order of the day. The *dargah* of Ghazi Mian, a Muslim saint of Benares, was visited by several devout Hindu Brahmin Kathaks.

Abdul Halim Sharar, whose earlier years were spent with Nawab Wajid Ali Shah, is also on record to say that Ayodhya and Varanasi were the centres of the Brahmin Kathaks. This is evident in the temples of Ayodhya coming alive during *sawan jhoola* with the *nritya sewa* of Kathaks in various temples, a practice that can still be seen. Herein also lies the importance of the small *tehsil* of Handiya, the home of the forefathers of the Lucknow *gharana* of Kathaks, for Handiya *tehsil* is strategically located between Allahabad (69 km from Handiya) and Varanasi (85 km from Handiya). Faizabad which was the capital of the *subedari,* is about 190 km north of Handiya. It made sense for them to go to Awadh to seek patronage.

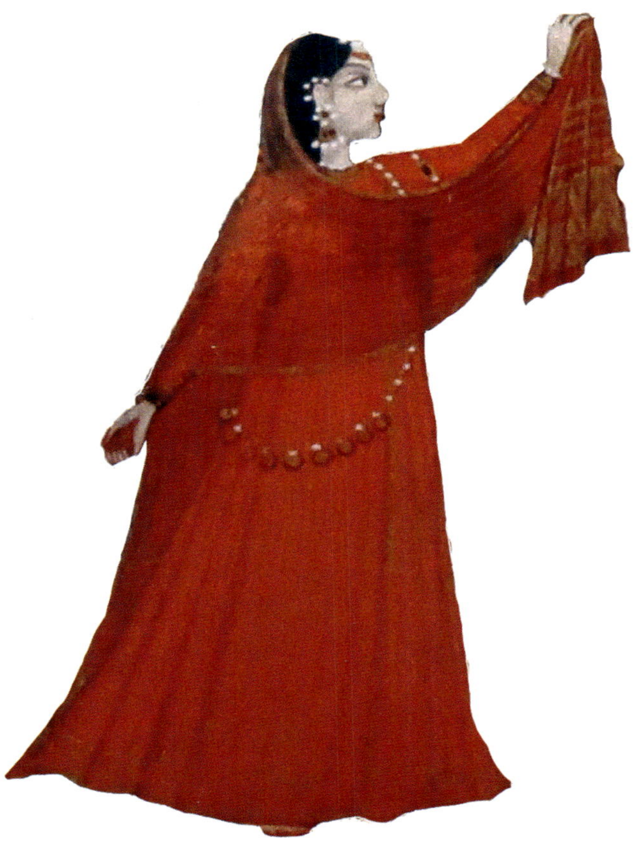

This therefore brings us to the next issue of why the Kathaks were considered part of high Hindu culture by the Muslims. Kathaks or the Kathak community or the Kathak Log were entrusted with the task of spreading moral and religious values to people who were not entitled to learn the scriptures or listen to a discourse on *dharma.* The narrative by the *kathak* or the *kathakar* (storyteller) was to be delineated through an audio-visual medium that appealed straight to the heart. This was called *kanta sammit updesh,* distinct from *vyas sammit updesh* and *suhrid sammit updesh.* The first direct epigraphic reference to Kathak as a community of Brahmins who sermonized through the medium of music and dance is from the Prakrit inscription of the fourth century BCE. This early Mauryan period Prakrit inscription throws light on the devotional dance of the Kathaks performing a *stuti* at Varanasi that pleased Lord Adinath, indicating the form of dance, the community of dancers and the region of the Gangetic belt. This was logical as the performing Kathaks were categorized as *dharak* Kathaks. References to Kathaks in the Adiparva, Anushasanaparva and Sabhaparva of the *Mahabharata* indicate their high caste and social status.

कथकाशचापरे राजन् श्रमनश्च वनौकसः
दिव्याख्यानानि ये चापि पठन्ति मधुरम द्विजाः
– महाभारत, आदिपर्व

Belonging to the Brahmin caste was an important factor for social acceptance in a caste-ridden society. This was later corroborated by the census of 1814 by Buchanan, in 1825 by James Princep and in 1891 by William Crooke and the report of Munshi Bhagwandas to a survey conducted at the behest of the colonial masters, that categorically stated that the Kathak performers either belonged to the sub-strata of Kanyakubj Brahmins or Gaur Brahmins. The hereditary practitioners of the Kathak of the Lucknow Gharana are Kanyakubj Brahmins.

The high esteem that the Kathaks enjoyed is evident from the fact that large land grants were given to them so much so that several villages by the name of Kathak had sprung up in different parts of central and eastern Uttar Pradesh and Bihar. The Brahmin Kathaks therefore fulfilled an important role in the dissemination of religious precepts and texts through a medium that appealed emotionally. They thus played a powerful role spreading values and shaping attitudes, opinions and behaviour, because people placed their trust in them. Dr Rishiraj Pathak, Asst Professor, University of Delhi, explains:

> The Kathaks use not only *kavya, sangeet* and *abhinaya* as a medium of expressing *kanta sammit updesh*, but that they use a beautiful and potent combination of all these constituents which produces the most beautiful *rasa* that helps the audience internalize the message of the text and which is the ultimate aim.

Thus it is understandable to see why and how the Kathaks were given a special place by both Hindu courts and the court of Awadh. On the special position of the Kathaks in Hindu courts, one has to turn to the thirteenth-century *Sangeet Ratnakara*, verse 1348, that distinguishes Kathaks from the various categories of dancers such as *nata, nartak, charan, vaitalik, kolhatik* and *perini* and gives them prime importance in the royal protocol along with *vagyakar*s, viz. *bandina, vidyavant* and *priyamvada*.

Kathaks are distinguished from the other three categories of *vagyakars,* because while all were learned men using speech and even song to get their message across to the audience, it was only the Kathaks who had the additional element of dance that along with their skill in verse and music created *bhava* which evoked *rasa* in the audience.

कथकाबन्दिनश्चात्तविद्यावन्त प्रियंवदाः
प्रशन्साकुशलश्चान्येचतुराः सर्वमातुशु ॥1348॥

Culturally, the brief rule of Nawab Wajid Ali Shah is considered to be the golden period of Lucknow's cultural history as dancers, poets and musicians regained their lost grandeur under his patronage. Wajid Ali was a musician, poet and dancer and he received training in Kathak as a *ganda-bandh shagird* from Durga Prasad, the illustrious son of Prakashji Maharaj. Even though belonging to the Shia branch of the Islamic faith, Nawab Wajid Ali Shah not only became a disciple of a Hindu Kanyakubj Brahmin Kathak, he was also influenced by the *rasadhari* performers and the *rasleela*s of Vrindaban. He is accredited with having staged many operas and dance-dramas. *rahas* productions were based on the lines of the *rasleela* and were choreographed in the Kathak style. More than thirty-six Rahas productions were staged during his brief rule Lucknow. He participated in the cast of a *yogi* in saffron robes in the *rahas* productions. These festivities centred on Hindu mythologies and came to be known as Jogiya Jashan. Several dancers received training in music and dance in the Parikhana established by the Nawab. As recorded by Adeeb in *Lucknow ka Shahi Stage*, the task of training the dancers (*paris*) fell to masters which Adeeb refers to as *ustad*s.

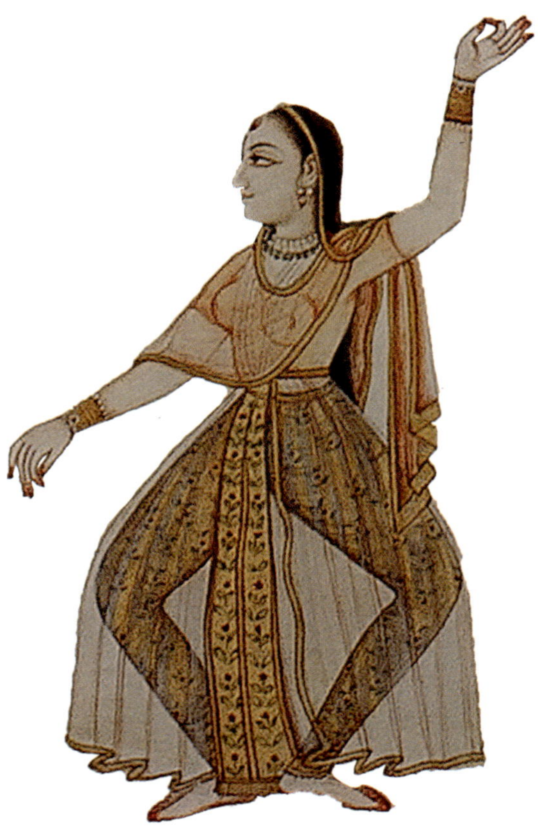

*sab pariyon ko teyyar karnaa*
*is fan ke ustaadon ka kaam hai.*
the task of teaching the girls is
that of the great masters of dance.

During Nawab Wajid Ali Shah's period, the dance-drama *Indra Sabha* (The Court of Lord Indra), was staged in 1853 and it was the first musical play in Urdu. It bears a remarkable resemblance to the *Vikramorvashiya*, *Radha Kanhaiyya ka Qissa* and similar works which were written, produced and staged with great pomp and splendour and which had Wajid Ali in the lead roles of Lord Indra and Lord Krishna respectively. While *Indra Sabha* along with a few other *rahas* performances was staged for the public (*awami*) stage there were other productions that were staged in the courts for a very select audience (*shahi*) stage.

Due to lack of exposure, the nouveau riche of Lucknow and the newly-rich *taluqdar*s were not so comfortable with the gravity and beauty of *dhrupad* style of music and preferred the lighter *thumri*. Although *thumri* as a musical genre is relatively new, the fifteenth-century treatise *Sangeet Damodar* speaks of a music composition *jhumri*, the precursor of *thumri* as follows:

*prayah sringarbahuta*
*madhvikamadhura mriduh*
*ekaiva jhumarirloke*
*varnadiniyamonjhita*
There is only one
composition in the world, viz.
*jhumri* which is mostly full of
erotic love,
sweet as *mahua* wine, soft
and free from the rules
regarding syllables on
metrics.

Since *thumri* in Brajbhasha, the dialect of Awadh area that evolved from Shauraseni Prakrit, was imbued with *shringar rasa* and was largely from the female perspective, hence increasing number of poet-musicians, both Hindus and Muslims, started composing *thumri*s depicting the *viraha* (longing of a woman) for her beloved. They became symbols for *atma* (soul) longing for union with the *paramatma* (the Absolute). These compositions reflected *shringar rasa* both in *viyog* (separation) and in *sambhog* (union). This was immediately accepted by the courtesans of Lucknow as it better suited their performances.

Because of his interest in staging dance-dramas, Wajid Ali Shah found that the genre of *dhrupad* music did not go well with the kind of musical plays he favoured. He therefore patronized *thumri* for several reasons: it was lighter than the heavy and sombre temper of *dhrupad*; it had a romantic flavour, was emotional and lent itself easily to *bol banav* and *artha bhava*. The Kathak Log were quick to recognize the situation and included the *thumri ang* in their delineation. The *dhrupad ang* which had been the basic mainstay of the dance of the Kathak Log now saw itself in the background. This move was opposed by many in Lucknow as they felt that classical music was being degraded.

Having learnt Hindustani classical music from some of the great maestros of his time, Nawab Wajid Ali Shah developed and evolved several new *raga*s such as Jog, Juhi and Shah Pasand. Being a gifted poet and secular at heart, he wrote several *thumri*s on the subject of Radha and Krishna under the pen name Akhtar Piya. One of his *thumri*s goes as follows:

*mohan rasiya aaye bagiya,*
*jhoom rahi ras kali kali re,*
*koi kali hari naam pukare,*
*koi kali sun ali ali re.*
When fun loving
Mohan enters the
garden
Each bloom started to
dance
Some blossom spoke
the name of Hari
other sang the one of
Ali

Another verse written by him is as follows:

*karna nath gajpat*
*hari, harpat gajpat*
*padpat gopal*
*akhtar jan dil ke*
*chain tumse, sach*
*man laga hai harilal.*
Oh Gopal! You are
the benevolent form
of Ganesha, Vishnu and
Shiva;
my life and mind bows before you in devotion.

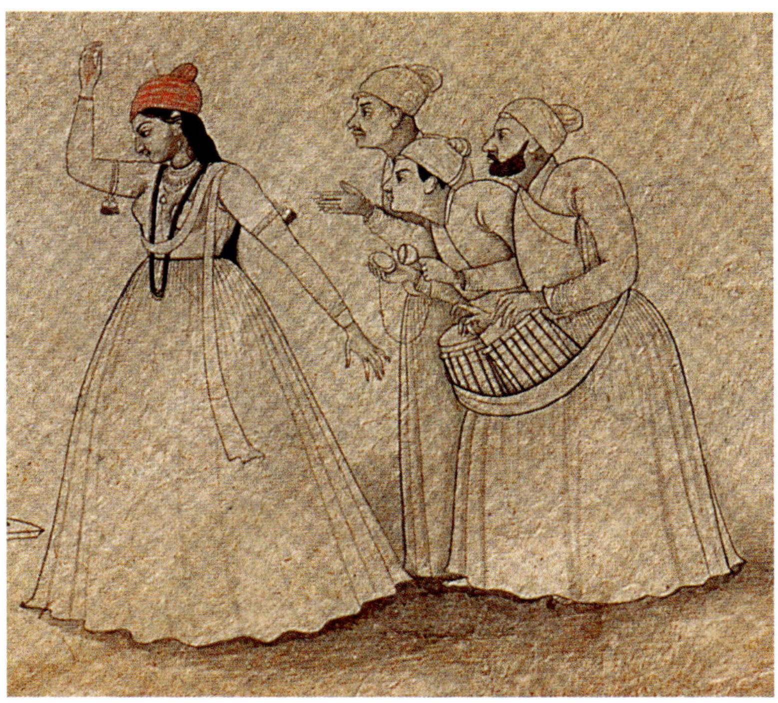
*Kathak dancer in a court, nineteenth[th] century*

His other compositions reflect secular influences as there are references to Holi and the Jhoola. But perhaps his most poignant verse is one which he wrote when leaving his beloved Lucknow after being exiled to Calcutta by the British.

*babul mora naihar chhooto ri jaye*
O my father! I am leaving home.

During the time of Wajid Ali Shah the *mridang*, which had been the staple accompaniment of *dhrupad* had to yield way to the *tabla* whose tone was lighter and more suited to the temperament of *thumri*.

Nawab Wajid Ali Shah is fondly remembered in the annals of music and dance not only as a great patron but also as a sensitive poet and a proficient Kathak, despite his bulky girth, who danced the *thaat ang* with precision, sensitivity and grace. Furthermore, though the Nawab ruled for a short period, from 1847 to 1856, yet he laid the foundation of patronization of Kathak, and also the formalization and stylization of the art form. His two books *Banni* and *Najo* have dwelt upon several techniques associated with the dance of the Kathak Log and the *gat-nikas* with illustrations. The *gat*s have been enumerated in *Banni* and some, enumerated in *Gunch-e-Raga* and *Saut-ul-Mubarak*, are from the *Natyashastra*, *Abhinaya Darpan*, *Sangeet Ratnakar* and *Nartan Nirnaya*, which only shows that Wajid Ali Shah was conversant with these texts and that he was also influenced by his teacher Pandit Durga Prasad.

Wajid Ali Shah is known for the performances of *rahas* which include several delineations of the *gats* of Kathak. It has been said that:

*un mein mausiqui*
*kam hai*
*aur mukhtalif aazaa*
*ki harkat-o-saknaat*
*zyada hain*
*yaani wo sirf raks ki*
*mukhtalif sooratein*
*hain.*
there is less display
of technicalities as
compared to display
of movements.

What is also interesting to note is the Persianization of Sanskrit terms that was used by the Kathak Log. In this context, Adeeb has recorded the following.

*puraane naamon mein beshtar ye*
*tagayyur kar diya gaya hai*
*ki hindi lafzon ki jagah un ke*
*ham-adhani farsi ya*
*arabi lafz rakh diye gaye hain*
*maslan "mor pankhi ki jagah taaus pankhi*
*aur sooraj mukhi ki jagah aftab mukhi". ...*
It is decreed that Sanskrit terms may be replaced
by Persian terms such as *mor pankhi* should
henceforth be called *taus pankhi* and *sooraj*
*mukhi* should be replaced by *aftab mukhi*. ...

This points to the presence and proficiency of Persian in the court of Wajid Ali Shah.

Nawab Wajid Ali Shah's interest extended to choreography too where he paid great attention to the placement of the dancer and the manner in which they entered the stage. His entry in the *Indra Sabha* had to be heralded with the sound of drums and vibration of his bracelets.

It is to the credit of Nawab Wajid Ali Shah and the well-known Kathak maestros of his time for their efforts in formalizing the *margi* or a more refined and courtly presentation of Kathak. In its transformation from a temple dance in the court of Wajid Ali Shah Kathak became a classical dance form. The *vardhamanak* was formalized to *rangmanch pravesh* which included the *salami*. Every aspect of the presentation, like the initial salutation, the *abhinaya*, footwork, pirouettes and the final climax, was regularized. At the same time, the traditional *rangmanch ki puja* was not lost sight of. Such formalization saw the dance of style as aesthetic refinement and grace became the fulcrum of presentation. Emphasis on the graceful execution of each *karana* and the beauty of body lines became important aspects in the aesthetics of the Lucknow Gharana. While the complete *bol*s were to be executed with feet, the lines of the hands, the angle of the body, the manner in which the eyes moved with the hand movement, the tilt of the face associated with the *karana* and the use of *recak*s of the hand, wrists, waist and neck became points of concentration that imparted a beautiful and distinctive flavour to the Kathak of Lucknow Gharana.

With the advent of Muslim rule, sociocultural changes had come about with the introduction of the *purdah* system. Various kinds of drawing the

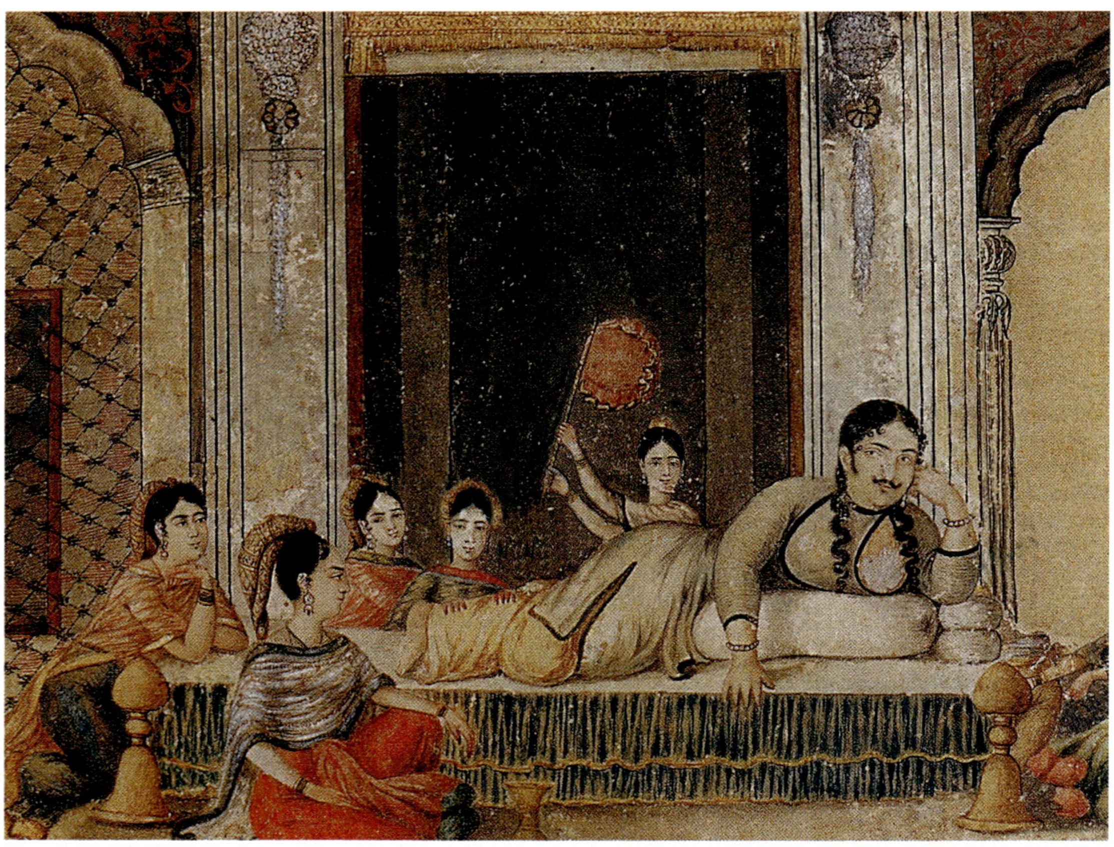

*Nawab Wajid Ali Shah along with gopis. Painted in his own time.*

the Kathak Log now being recognized as Kathak dance, derived from the name of the Kathak community, and which laid the foundations of the Lucknow Gharana.

With the interest and patronage extended by Nawab Wajid Ali Shah, coupled with the etiquettes of his court, a distinctive style developed that later became the hallmarks of the Lucknow Gharana. Awadh was known for elegance, grace, pomp and splendour, distinct from the virile and strong approach of the Kathak performers of Rajasthan. Therefore, in the Lucknow Gharana, the placement of feet was close to each other and lifting of legs was usually avoided. This approach lent a graceful slide to the *charis*. Subtlety, *haav-bhava*, *harakat* and *nazakat* became important parts of the Lucknow

*ghunghat* with associated glances, *drishti bhava* and several extended applications of the original *gati*s were added to the repertoire of *gat nikas.* Hindi literature of Ritikaal also influenced the furtherance of *gat*s as the gaits depicted the state of the woman in love. The feminine gaits *gat*s were known as *zenana nirat* and the masculine *gat*s were known as *mardana nirat*. These popular terminologies seem to have been in vogue from the time of Emperor Akbar but were improved in the time of Wajid Ali Shah.

The text of *thumri* centred on the legends of Krishna and Radha. While emoting, emphasis was on nuanced expressions of the text and on myriad interpretations of a word or line of a text. The element of *upaj* (improvisation), both in the rhythmic field as well as in *abhinaya*, is perhaps the strongest in Kathak. *Upaj* in *abhinaya* is best demonstrated in the *bhava batana* where each line or each word is interpreted in myriad ways. This led to its full flowering under the dancers of Lucknow Gharana. The delicacy and finesse with which *bhava,* expression of the text of the song, was rendered through *nayan-bhava* (through the media of eyes and pupil), *bol-bhava* (symbolic interpretations), *artha-bhava* (interpreting the meaning of the text in various ways), *nritya-bhava* (using dance movements and patterns along with the interpretation) and *gat-artha-bhava* (where each movement and gait was used to convey a sentiment) and the extent to which referential (*avidha*), metaphorical (*lakshana*) and poetic interpretations of the text (*vyanjana*), became hallmarks of this *gharana.*

A legend associated with Shambhu Maharaj goes as follows:

> While enacting out *mohe chhedo mat, jaane do kanha* (tease me not, let me go Kanha), wherein each word and each phrase was sung and enacted out in various ways, Maharaj suddenly, with a pause, changed the emphasis to *mohe chhedo, mat jaane do kanha* (tease me, do not let me go Kanha) and which had the audience marvel at the flight of imagination and immediate *upaj.*

The *ishta-devata* of the Bindadin Maharaj family is Lord Krishna and hence all *abhinaya* sequences of this *gharana* are largely Krishna based. Bindadin Maharaj was a prolific writer and his *thumri*s are the mainstay of the Lucknow Gharana of Kathak. It is because of Bindadin Maharaj's exceptional gift as a poet that *thumri*s in Brajbhasha became the mainstay of Kathak in Lucknow. Most of the dancers of the Lucknow Gharana were adept at singing too. In fact Shambhu Maharaj is on record to say that singing was essential for rendering *abhinaya* as it provided its soul.

As regards *kavitt ang*, the emphasis of the Lucknow Gharana Kathak is to enact the verse while it is sung in the *nibaddh* style. There is a view that when recited as rhythmic pattern, the *kavitt* seems to replicate drum syllables like *dha*, *ge* and *na* which is considered disrespectful. In contrast, in the Jaipur Gharana, enactment of a *kavitt* is to the recitation of the text in *madhya laya,* indicative of the *vacikabhinaya* of the *Natyashastra*. The *prahelika kavitt* seeks to find interpretations and clues for a given situation thus calling upon the imagination of the poet or the performer. This particular *prahelika kavitt* which is performed in both the *gharana*s as a rhythmic utterance, has a legend associated with Bindadin Maharaj. According to a legend, Nawab Wajid Ali Shah asked the gathering of poets, musicians and dancers to give their interpretations as to why the *nayika*'s palms were found to be burnt. While most of the interpretations centred round her inexperience in cooking, it was young Bindadin who improvised and interpreted that it was the modesty of the young bride, beset with mixed emotions of joy, fear and curiosity that led to such a situation. On being undressed by her husband, her shame and modesty make her cover the flame of the wick lamp with her palms that results in the burns.

*nai abala rasa reet na jaane,*
*sej chaddhi jiya maahe dari,*
*rasa baat kahi, tab chonk pari,*
*tab dahe ke kandhan baanh dhari,*
*in dono ke jhakjhoran mein,*
*katinar pitambar toot pari,*
*kar deepak se tan dhaank liyo,*
*jin kaaran sunder haath jali.*

The naive young bride sitting on the bed was startled when he whispered words of love. She struggled hard to get away from his passionate embrace but in the ensuing struggle her clothes loosened. Mortified, she tried to cover her modesty by covering the oil-lamp, the one and only witness, and thus burnt her palms.

The *nritta* sequences, viz. the pure rhythmic patterns of the Lucknow school, boasts of simplicity, clarity, precision and finesse in execution. Thus, while both the Jaipur and Lucknow *gharana*s do emphasize rhythmic excellence in the *nritta ang*, yet the emphasis placed on *tipalli, chaupalli paran*s in the Jaipur Gharana is largely absent in the Lucknow Gharana. Furthermore, certain rhythmic phrases such as *tram thai thai ta thai thai ta thai* and *gheghe ghegbe ghegbe tita*, which are common occurrences in the Jaipur Gharana, are not used in the Lucknow Gharana. Demystification of some of the most difficult rhythmic patterns which laid the foundations of *ginati ki tihai*s (*tihai*s executed to numerals) resulted in as some by-products of the Lucknow Gharana.

Another legend associated with the rhythmic wizardry of the *nritta ang* in the Lucknow Gharana again pertains to young Bindadin Maharaj who was otherwise known for his poetic and *abhinaya* skills. It is believed that in a challenge thrown by a well-known *mridang* player, Kodau Singh, the ageing Durga Prasadji, father of young Bindadin, was anxious. However Bindadin saved the family name as he performed non-stop for several hours to the accompaniment of Kodau Singh's *pakhawaj* where his feet and hands became a virtual blur as the speed kept increasing. At one moment, for a split second, Kodau Singh faltered out of momentary tiredness and this led to the seven-year old Bindadin winning the day, thus saving his family's reputation. The preference for the *tabla* over *mridang* led to an emphasis on the rhythmic patterns based on the *tabla* and dance syllables which, in turn, led to the *natwari ang* of Kathak. This period also saw the practice of question and answer (*sawal–jawab*) between the dancer and the percussionist and the flowering of rhythmic melodic compositions such as the *tarana*.

On the issue of costumes, even though the costume of the people of the Gangetic belt, viz. namely *lehenga–choli* and *dhoti–bandi* continued to hold sway, yet there was an increased association of donning the *angarakha–churidar*. It is worthwhile to remember that the *angarakha–churidar* costume was indigenous to India since third century BCE as is evident from the sculptures of dance from ancient India of third century and fifth century CE. References to both kinds of costumes have also been made in tenth century by Al-Beruni, chronicler of Mahmud of Ghazni, in his description of costumes worn in Hindu India.

Because of the outstanding achievements and contributions to the field of Kathak and also having over hundred disciples, the title of *maharaj* (king among kings) was bestowed on the most outstanding Kathak *guru* of Asaf-ud-Daulah's court. It was respect for the eminent Brahmin Kathaks and their skills that the mandatory *topi* (head covering) was not insisted upon by the Muslim rulers of Awadh.

In the annals of Indian cultural history, the period eighteenth to the twentieth centuries was of great importance for it defined the renaissance of Indian art and culture. In this context, when speaking of the Lucknow Gharana and its hallmarks, it is necessary to go back in time to understand its evolution for it was the socio-political development of the preceding eras that laid the foundations of this *gharana*. By late nineteenth century, the influence of Lucknow and that of Jaipur had become significant and therefore at a conference in 1895 it was decided to speak of the styles according to its place of patronage. Thus, the styles of performance of the Ishwari Prasad family of Lucknow and that of Bhanu Prasadji of Jaipur came to be recognized as the Lucknow Gharana and the Jaipur Gharana respectively.

Pandit Birju Maharaj, alias Brij Mohan Mishra, son of Pandit Acchhan Maharaj, has taken Kathak to new heights. Having lost his father at the tender age of nine, he was trained by his two uncles Lacchhu Maharaj and Shambhu Maharaj, imbibing the best from both. He is considered to be the true representative of the Lucknow Gharana as his dance bespeaks of immense grace, *nazakat*, *harakat*, technical and rhythmic brilliance, breathtaking *upaj ang* combined with mastery over singing, playing of drums and instrumental music as well as inheriting the poetic genius of his grand-uncle, Bindadin Maharaj.

Today, in an ever-changing environment, while maintaining its hallmark, there is nonetheless, a pragmatic evolution of the style of the Lucknow Gharana. What is of great importance that in this era, while newer avenues of expression, themes, costumes and presentations have become features of innovative process in dance the stamp and signature of Pandit Birju Maharaj still prevails. The spirit and ethos of the Lucknow Gharana, namely its emphasis on grace and aesthetics, are bywords that continue to be followed. The sermonizer Brahmin, the Kathak, continues to live through the performers of this *gharana* and continues to nurture and nourish the rich classical heritage of the country as also of this very ancient art form with a recorded history of over 2,500 years.

Lucknow shone like a diamond in the cultural scenario of Awadh, a culture that reflected inter-disciplinary dialogues, mutual respect and syncretism. It gifted the world of classical dance, the well-known Lucknow Gharana of Kathak dance. Today, a sense of nostalgia engulfs many who visit Lucknow: monuments with Islamic and British Raj era architecture, rumbling facades of old buildings, the hustle bustle of Hazratganj and the soft-spoken old timer *rickshawala*s and *paanwala*s, all of which exude fragrance of faded grandiosity. One almost hears a whisper saying:

अधूरा किस्सा लिखकर पन्ने मोड़ आया हूँ।
खुद का एक टुकड़ा लखनऊ छोड़ आया हूँ॥

Incomplete written pages
have I left behind half folded,
And with it in Lucknow,
I have left behind a part of myself.

**Reference**

Sharar, Abdul Halim, 2001, *Lucknow: The Last Phase of an Oriental Culture: Dance and Development of the Kathak School*, pp. 141-42, New Delhi: Oxford University Press.

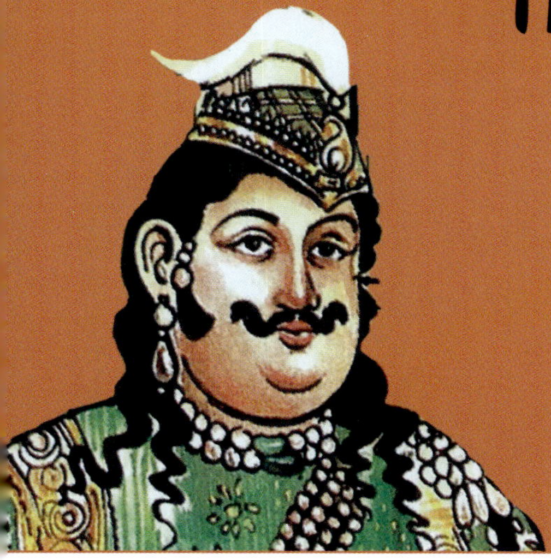

# The Poet and His Poetry

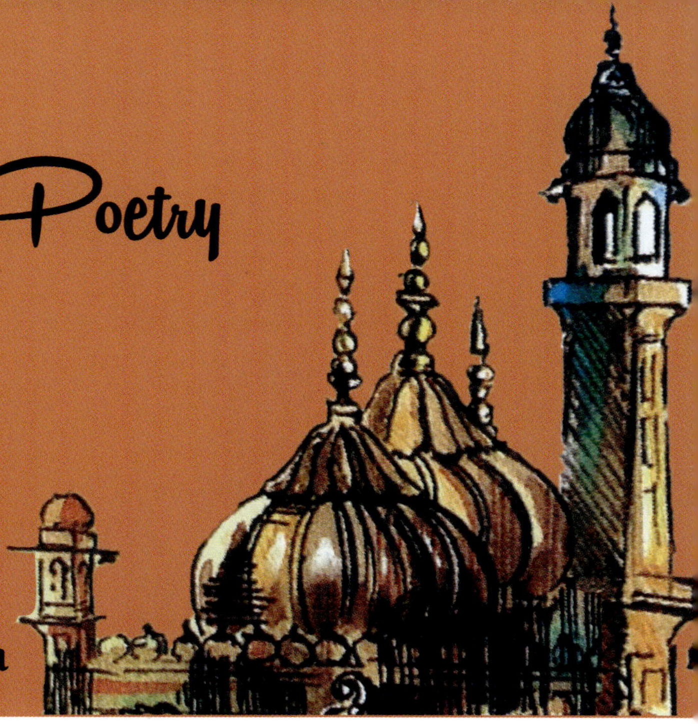

**Harsha V. Dehejia**

To write about Nawab Wajid Ali Shah one would need a *kalam* of honey, *nupur*s that sing love songs, *kavi*s whose words can capture the hushed words of *shringar rasa* in the *pranaya mandap*, *chitrakar*s who can paint the charmed ambience of the court and the conversations of the courtiers, *sangeetkar*s who can play the sweetest notes of *raga*s of love, *nartaki*s who can emulate the romance of the *gopi*s of Vrindavana and *sutra*s that can whisper sensuous words from costumes that befit such a romantic situation. In short, Wajid Ali Shah as a connoisseur and practitioner of the arts, was a remarkable person and his court a charmed space alive with the pleasures of amour. Our interest stops there, for we are not here to evaluate his administrative skills as a *nawab*, for better or worse, that was already done by the East India Company. We take our stand on Wajid Ali Shah as an artist and a *rasik* and his contribution to the world of art.

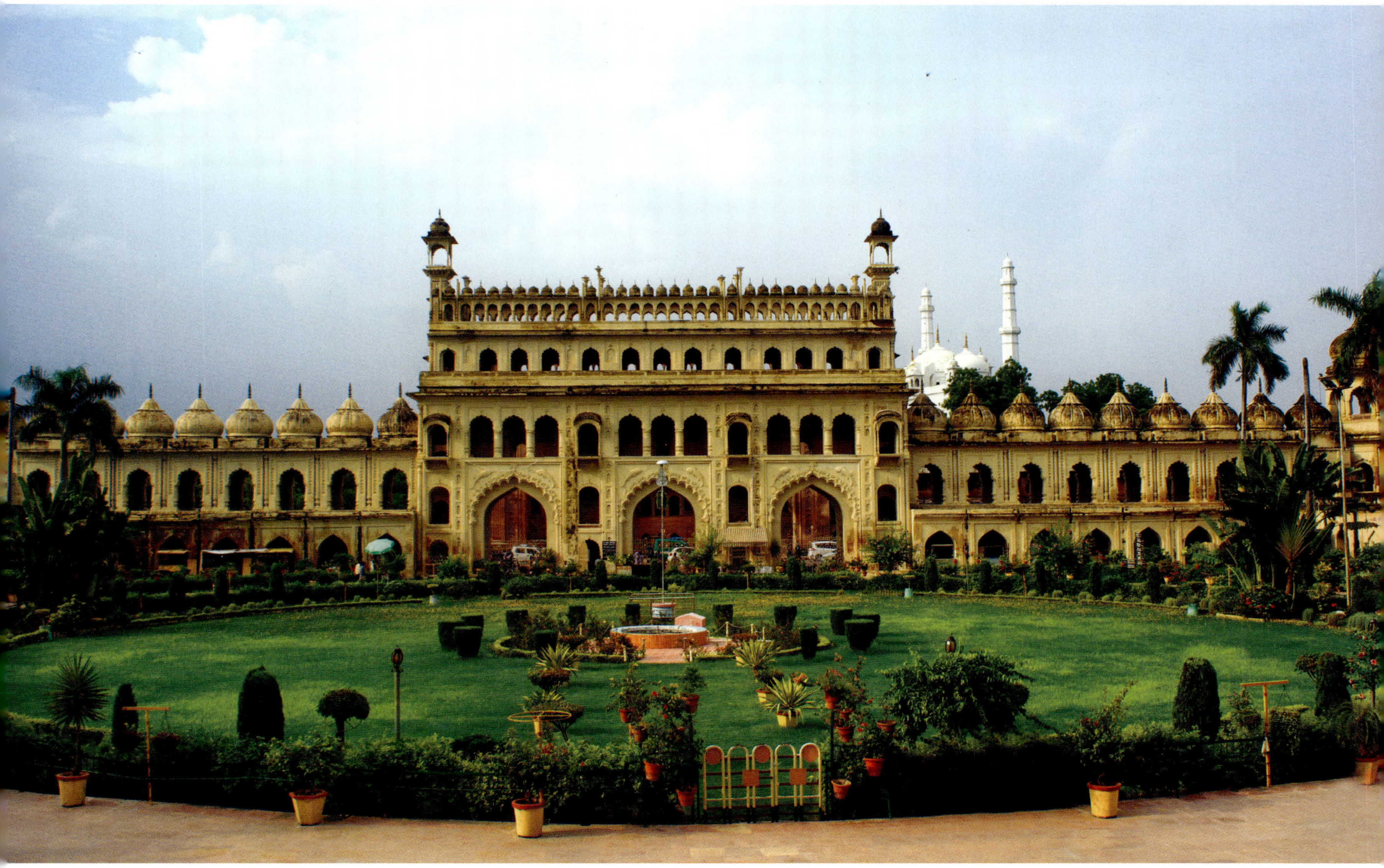

*Bada Imambara*

There were many factors that contributed to the emergence of Awadh as the centre of the manifold arts in the nineteenth century. The power and glory of the Mughals were fading, the *kathakars* (storytellers) in many regions of the Hindi belt like Ayodhya and Benares were looking for safer pastures and patrons as the dominance of the Muslims was difficult to deal with, *dhrupad* as a musical genre had seen better days and was replaced by *thumri* as the preferred musical mode, the romantic poetry of Ritikaal which started with Keshavdas in Orchha in the sixteenth century and replaced Sanskrit with Brajbhasha as the language of choice for romantic poetry and this was celebrated in homes and *havelis* and created many shades and colours of *nayikas* all of which made the Muslim *nawabs* in this predominantly Hindu region connoisseurs of arts of *shringar*. This was the perfect setting for Wajid Ali Shah to emerge as the royal *shringar rasa nayak*.

It was not difficult for Wajid Ali Shah to cross over from his Shia background to the predominantly Hindu culture of Awadh. He was a gifted poet, who wrote under the *takhullas* of Akhtar (the star). He wrote love poetry, often about his own amorous affairs with the beauties of his court or *paris* (fairies) as he called them. He also composed *thumris*, love songs expressing romantic longing, and popularized them in his court, writing under the name of Kadar Piya.

Llewellyn Jones is correct in observing:

> In Muslim culture, which has no history of theatre, the story-tellers (*kathakars*) fulfilled the need for dramatic narrative, with hand gestures and facial expressions. When instrumental and vocal music was added the Kathak performer was able to act out stories with stylized mime (and this led to the dance we call Kathak). The story of Radha and Krishna and other figures was retold now in dance form, characterized by rhythmic footwork and pirouettes, where the dancers' skirts would whirl out and the tinkling of their ankle bells accompany each stamp of their bare feet.

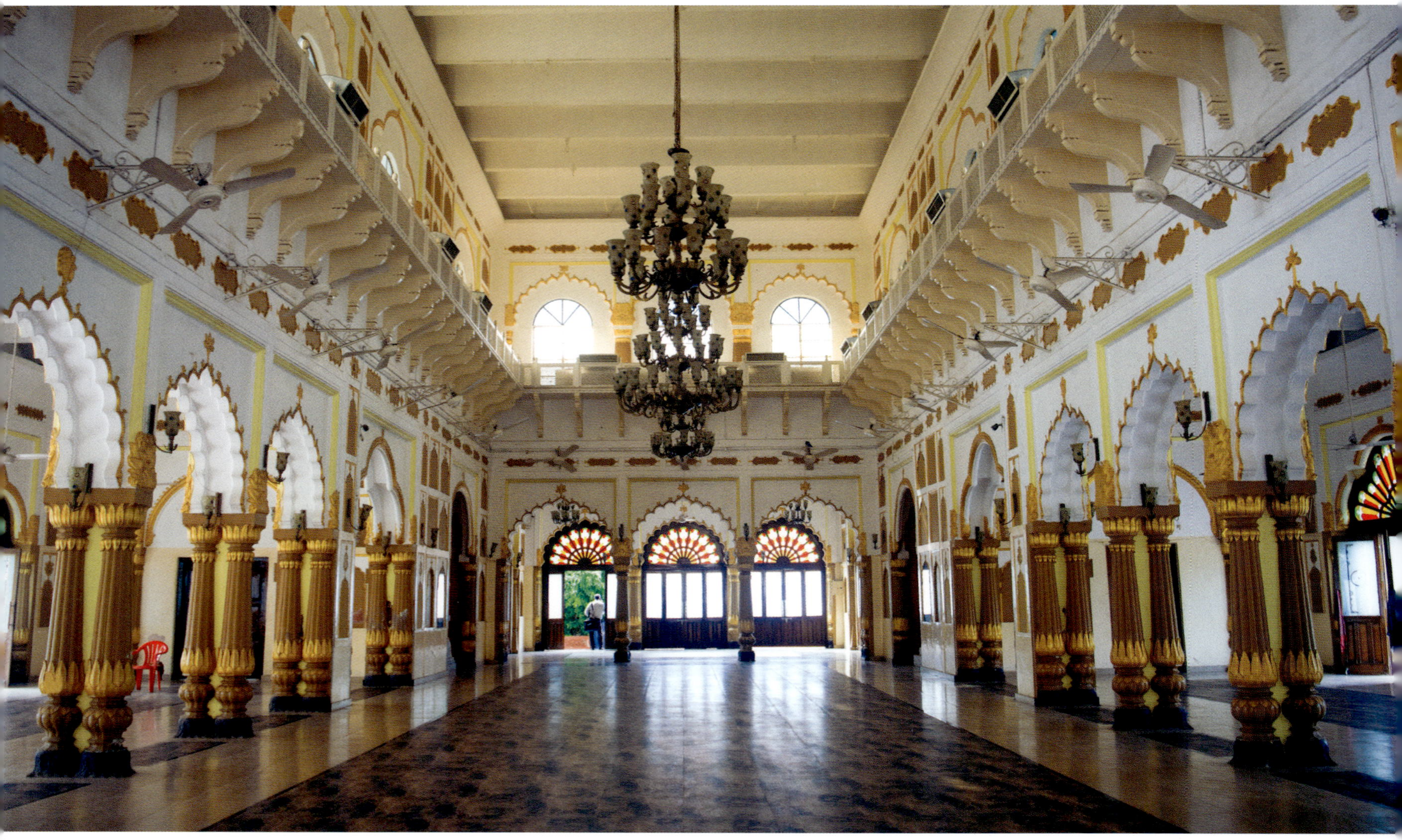

*Safed Baradari*

For Wajid Ali Shah this was an opportunity to indulge in the many expressions of *shringar* and *kathak* was the best representation of the same.

If the Mughal kings were known for their majestic architecture, Wajid Ali on his accession to the throne in 1847 lost no time in ordering a huge new palace, the Qaisarbagh, to be built. It was built in the grand baroque style with statues, ornamental canals and fountains. These structures in the time of Wajid Ali

Shah resonated with dance and music, poetry and drama, where Wajid Ali would preside and even participate.

Krishna-*leela* (the love games of Krishna), which were given a textual basis in the *Srimad Bhagavatam* and grew through the poetry of the *ashtachaap kavis* of Shrinathji, Jayadeva's *Gita Govinda*, the *kirtans* of Chaitanya and the evocative poetry of *ritikavis* like Keshavdas, Bihari, Sunder, Matiram and many others. This, rather than the Krishna theology of the *Bhagavadgita*, attracted both Hindus and Muslims, for it enabled them to participate in the many amorous sports of Krishna, without losing their religious or social identity. Rasa Khan, an Afghan Muslim, about a hundred years before Wajid Ali Shah, wrote movingly about Krishna-*leela* which earned him the title of a Muslim Vaishnava. Likewise, at about the same time, there were Muslims in Bengal who sang of the romantic Krishna and many of them had both Muslim and Hindu names. Wajid Ali Shah falls in the same genre as these poets.

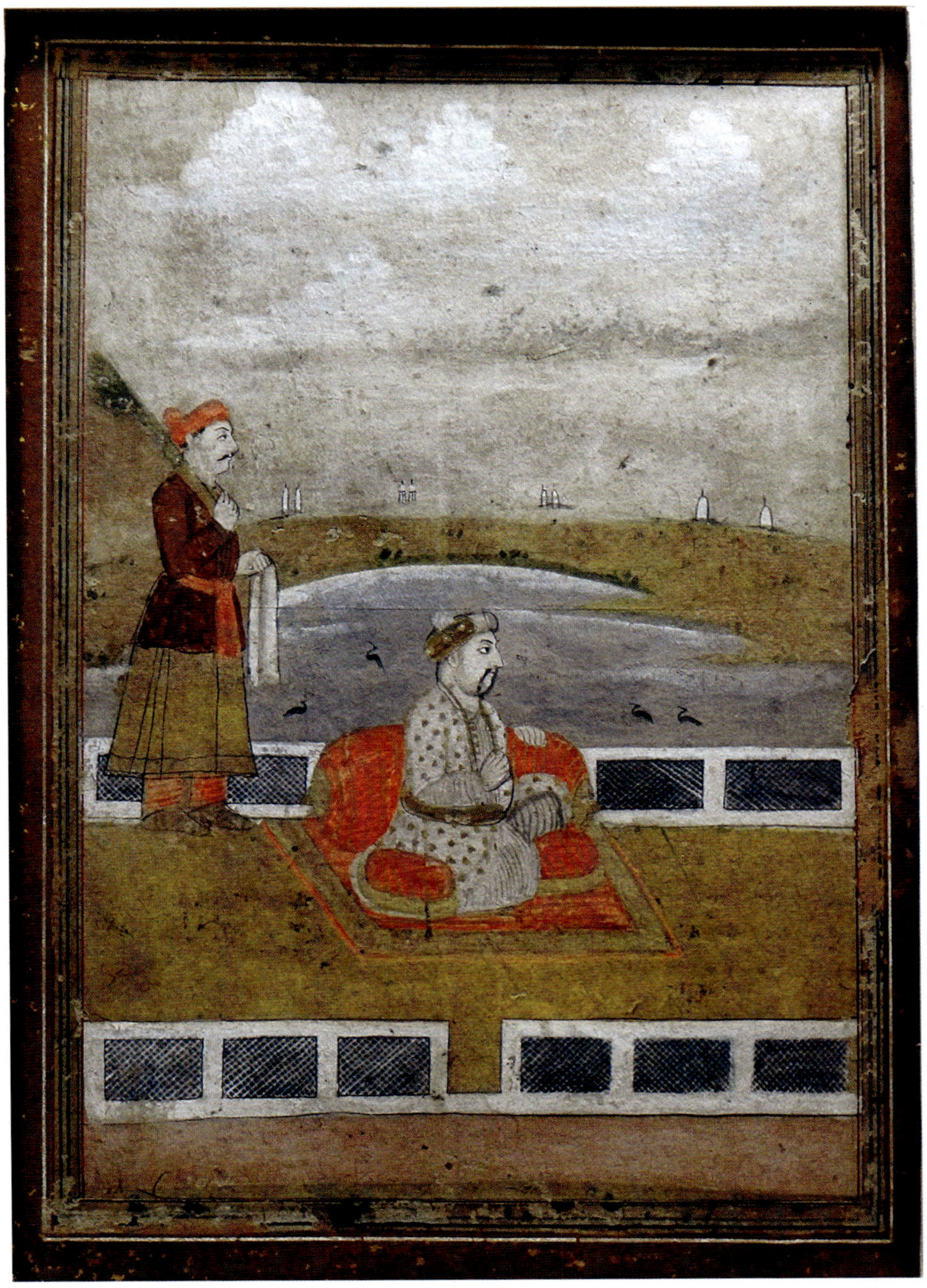

*Nawab Asaf-ud-Daulah, Awadh, c. 1830*

Wajid Ali Shah had seen the Rahas, the theatrical representations of Sri Krishna's dance, and was so pleased with Sri Krishna's amatory dalliances that he devised a drama about them in which he himself played the part of Krishna and the beautiful ladies of his palace acted as *gopis*. Very often there would be a street fair and ordinary people of the town were allowed to take part in these pastimes, but only on the condition that they came wearing clothes dyed in red ochre. The result was that even old men of eighty would put on red garments and become young sparks, filling the cups of their old age with the joyous wine of the king's youthfulness. In this respect Wajid Ali's court differed from that of the Mughals, for the latter the *diwan-i-khas* and the *diwan-i-aam* were to be kept distinct.

Wajid Ali Shah's exuberance for the celebration of Krishna-*leela* spilled over to the streets of Lucknow, where the singing of *thumris* and gathering of poets were common place and sounds of this could be heard till late into the night as people would gather in narrow streets savouring culinary delights.

Wajid Ali Shah was also a designer of clothes. His unique *kurta* was his own creation and he encouraged the art of *chickenkari*, a fabric art that thrives even today in Lucknow. As for the art of painting Wajid Ali did maintain a small atelier but the standard of painting came nowhere close to that of the Mughals. Portraiture was the preferred genre and very often Wajid Ali would like himself to be painted with all the preceding *nawabs* creating a visual tree as it were.

Wajid Ali presided over the last flicker of the grand majestic courts of medieval India where if a thousand pigeons filled the Lucknow sky during the day, a thousand *diyas* and hundreds of beautiful women recreated the amorous *leelas* of Krishna, where music and wine flowed and late into the night hushed conversations of courtiers mingled with the songs under a starry night. Wajid Ali Shah cannot easily be forgotten, he will have a pride of place in the pages of the history of *shringar rasa* and when one watches a Kathak performance today one's mind will surely hark back to his court and the sound of anklets will remind us that once lived a king for whom the expression of *shringar* was a royal calling.

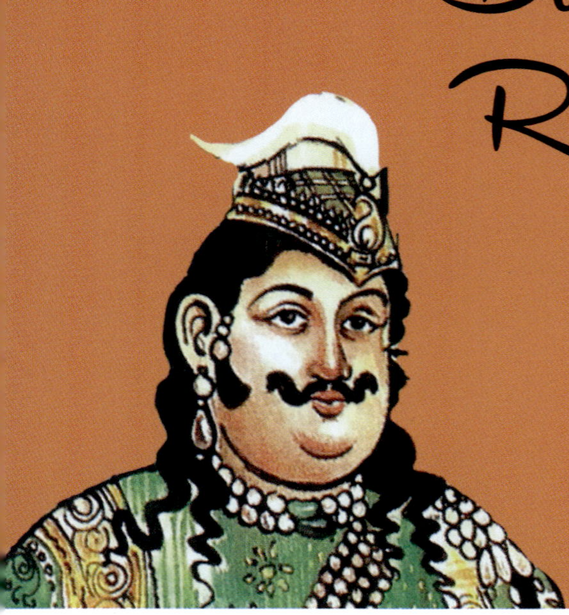

# Decadence or Connoisseurship?: Revisiting Wajid Ali Shah's Musical Scholarship

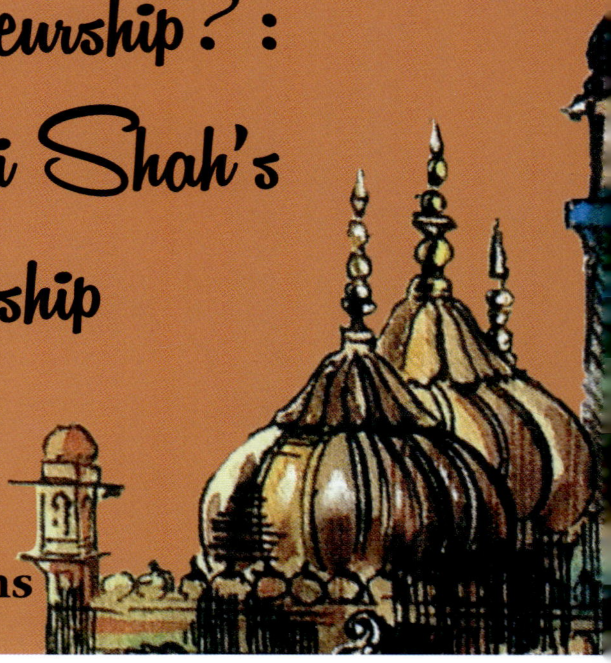

**Richard David Williams**

Wajid Ali Shah was a prolific scholar and a very productive self-publisher. By 1877, the king had written forty-six works, rising perhaps to one hundred before his death ten years later. From his exiled court in Matia Burj, he contributed to the literary life of Calcutta, disseminating books from his own printing press. However, today his works largely lie forgotten and Wajid Ali Shah is remembered primarily as a music enthusiast and only occasionally as an erudite intellectual.

This neglect is partly a question of language. Scholars writing in Urdu – most notably Kaukab Qadr Sajjad Ali Mirza and Masud Hasan Rizvi – have explored his works at length.[1] However, most people's memory of the Nawab has largely been shaped – directly or indirectly – by the Hindi and English translations of the essays by the Urdu journalist Abdul Halim Sharar (1860–1926). Sharar had spent a portion of his childhood in Matia Burj from 1869 to 1879, where his maternal grandfather Munshi Qamaruddin held an appointment in the administration between 1877 and 1879.[2] Sharar went on to become a popular novelist and journalist, his works including fifteen popular histories and twenty-eight historical novels.[3] Among his essays is a series of articles about the culture of Lucknow: these provide a rich, almost ethnographic account of Awadh before 1857, covering everything from pigeons to perfumes. Though Sharar himself never personally saw what he termed the *Lucknow of Old* (*Guzashta Lakhna'u*) his work hearkened back to the lost world of Islamicate Hindustan. The Calcutta court was mentioned sparingly, and only as a clone of Lucknow:

> From the time of the king's arrival in Calcutta, a second Lucknow had arisen in its neighbourhood. The real Lucknow had ended and was replaced by Matia Burj. ... No one thought he was in Bengal.[4]

By claiming that for thirty years the culture of Lucknow was impeccably preserved, Sharar crafted a romantic ideal of an authentic *nawabi* world, uncompromised by colonial modernity until its dissolution upon the death of Wajid Ali Shah.

Sharar characterized Lucknow as the apex of civilization in a bygone age. Etiquette and social graces came from royal courts: these alone were refined and cultured (*muhazzab aur sha'ista*).[5] Lucknow was the successor and better of Delhi, and the highest attainment of Indian culture (*tamaddun*): "All refined men from other regions now follow the ways of the citizens of Lucknow."[6] Following the loss of dominion in Awadh, according to Sharar's narrative, Lakhnavi culture could not advance further at Matia Burj, but only stagnate before ultimate dissolution.

Sharar's notion of a conclusive end to the development of Lakhnavi culture was particular to his work, and not shared by other cultural commentators, who suggested that certain *nawabi* customs and practices continued into the twentieth century.[7] Sharar neglected the persistence and evolution of the "old world" at Matia Burj and among the *ta'alluqadar*s of Awadh for rhetorical and stylistic reasons; as C.M. Naim has argued, "nostalgia becomes truly enjoyable to the nostalgic only when he manages somehow to convince himself that the 'golden' past was totally lost and for good".[8] Nostalgia was increasingly popular in Urdu literature in the early twentieth century, and Sharar had to euthanize *nawabi* culture in order to make it more appealing and tragic to his readers.

The essays on musical culture were highly influenced by Sharar's consultant, the musician Asadullah "Kaukab" Khan (*c.*1850–1919). Sharar and Kaukab were ideally suited collaborators, since they shared a similar experience of Lakhnavi culture. Kaukab had also known Matia Burj fleetingly as a child: his father, Niamatullah Khan (*c.*1816–1911) was attached to the court in the late 1860s but then proceeded to Kathmandu in the early 1870s, where he trained Kaukab and his older brother Karamatullah Khan (1848–1933). Kaukab was a highly educated Urdu litterateur in his own right and was preparing a treatment of music, the *Jauhar-i Musiqi* (1915), though he passed away before he could arrange for its publication. Like Sharar, Kaukab drew on the memories of his predecessors to fashion a memory of *nawabi* musical culture. Again, like Sharar, this memory was distilled through his contemporary misgivings about the position of Muslim civilization in early twentieth-century India, and by what he considered to be the decline of culture. Here, I will consider Kaukab's claims about Wajid Ali and court music, and assess their contribution to Sharar's vision for the legacy of Matia Burj.

**Dilettante or Connoisseur?**

Sharar cited at length from a letter in which Kaukab detailed musical life under the *nawabs*. Kaukab's overall argument was that music had flourished in the court in spite of Wajid Ali Shah, who had limited its potential by focusing on tawdry styles and forms.[9] His letter began by declaring that Wajid Ali conferred titles upon the less able musicians, to the neglect of experts; yet shortly after this, Kaukab contradicted himself, suggesting "whilst little interest was taken in pure classical music, expert musicians were much esteemed at the royal court". Kaukab added that the *nawab* "had been taught the science of music by Basit Khan and had a very good understanding of it. Being highly talented, the King had evolved new *raginis* to his own liking."[10] Kaukab was thus torn between two images of the king: as a superficial dilettante who did not recognize true artistry; or as an expert and innovator (trained by Niamatullah Khan's own *ustad*, and thus a *guru-bhai* of Kaukab's father).

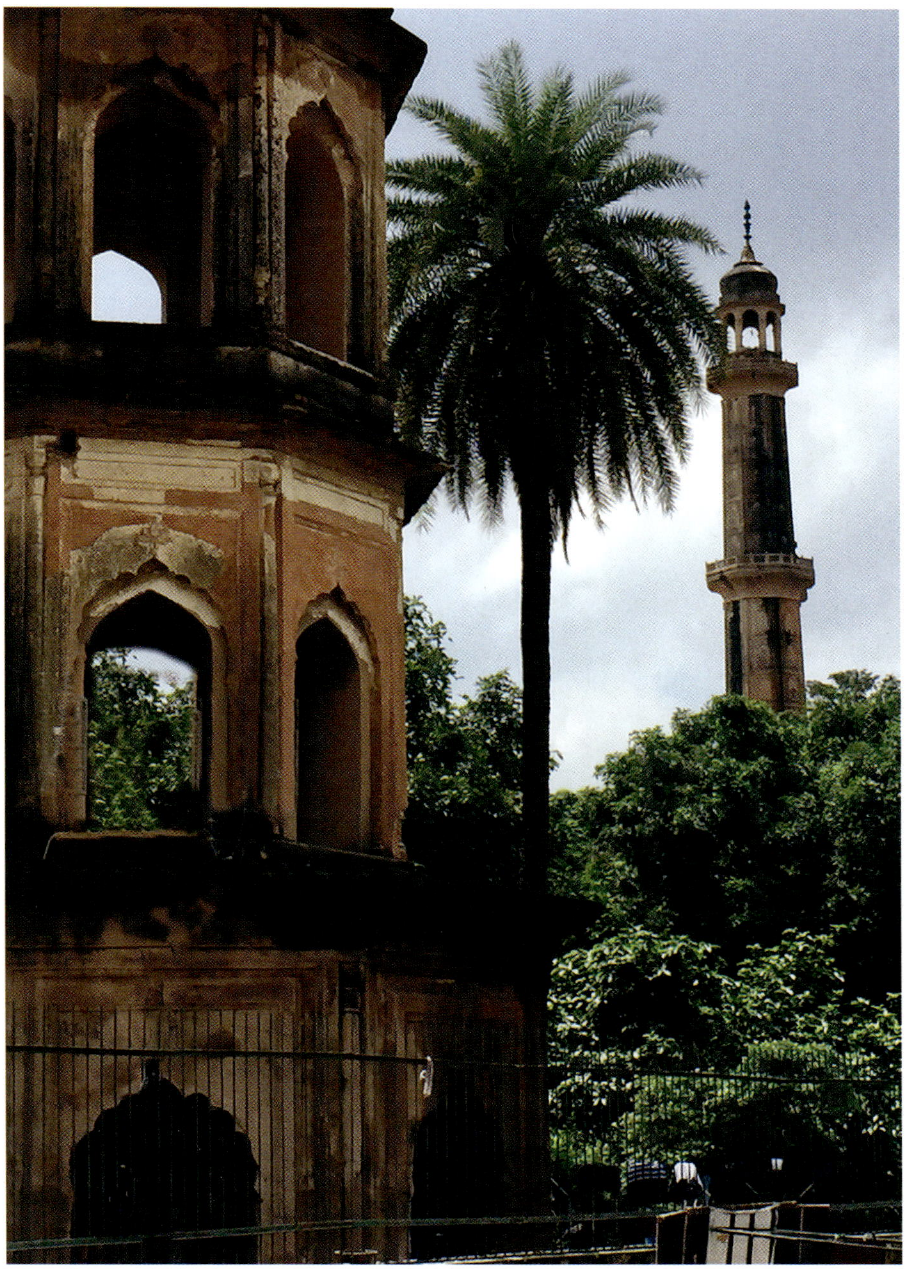

*Near Rumi gate, Lucknow*

Kaukab disapproved of Wajid Ali's innovations and was frustrated that a connoisseur so highly trained in aesthetic theory should make an informed decision to support seemingly tawdry music:

> Wajid Ali Shah was a master at the art and possessed the knowledge of an expert but he cannot escape the criticism that it was his conventional and cheap tastes that made the music of Lucknow frivolous and easily understandable by all. In accordance with popular tastes even the most discriminating singers omitted difficult techniques and based their music on light, simple, and attractive tunes which could be appreciated by every-one.[11]

Clearly a different critic might view this characterization (music as enjoyable and accessible) as a positive development. Kaukab was harsher in his own book: he charged Wajid Ali with neglecting musical knowledge, arguing that no reliable books on the art were written in his reign and that earlier key works on musicology – specifically the *Usul al-Naghmat-i asafi* (1793), the *Tohfat al-Hind* (*c.*1675), and the *Shams al-Aswat* (1698) – had been wholly neglected.[12] This criticism is evidence of Kaukab's serious underestimation of Wajid Ali's intellectual accomplishments.

Wajid Ali Shah himself composed and published at least five works on music. The first of these, *Saut al-Mubarak* (*Voice of the Blessed*) was written in Persian in Lucknow around 1852-53. Wajid Ali's introduction expressed his frustration with the existing literature on music: he had consulted several texts, including the *Usul al-Naghmat-i Asafi*, the *Khulasat al-'Aish-i 'Alam Shahi* (1798) and the *Sangitadarpana* (*c*.1600).[13] The first of these was named for its patron and Wajid Ali's predecessor Nawab Asafuddaulah (r.1775-97). In Wajid Ali's digest he skipped over the sections of music theory he thought redundant, preserving a chapter on *sur*, another on rhythm,[14] a brief discussion of instruments, and then three larger and wholly unprecedented chapters on dance (*raqs*), anecdotal stories (*naql*) and musical theatre (*rahas*). It was not that Wajid Ali was unread, as Kaukab suggested, but rather that he considered earlier scholarship inadequate:

> From my childhood I have felt attracted to music, but I did not acquire even a glimpse of its countenance. Those who are knowledgeable in this art are miserly and unambitious. ... Finally, I acquired this art, enchained to discipline and through mental struggle, and this book [*Saut al-Mubarak*] was written with the view to extending it to others.[15]

Kaukab may not have approved of Wajid Ali's approach, but it was inaccurate to accuse the *nawab* of neglecting his studies.

Many of Wajid Ali Shah's own works have not survived. Many were lost in 1857, and then again when the properties of Matia Burj were auctioned off thirty years later.[16] The libraries of Lucknow were looted during the uprising and many volumes were burned. Wajid Ali was personally aggrieved by this loss and composed a verse on "the pillage of vile men":

*ek hasrat haur par bhi bhar musi rah gayi*
*aisa kuch dekha ki ankhon ko tamnna rah gayi*
The rat filled itself up, even in a state of grief:
Seeing such things, the eyes retained their longing.[17]

This did not dissuade him from continuing his literary pursuits in Matia Burj, where he installed a printing press. He published several new works on music: two song anthologies, *Naju* (*Delicate Woman*, 1868)[18] and *Dulhan* (*Bride*, 1873),[19] a larger work named *Banni* (*Bride*, 1877), and then *Chanchal Nazanin* (*Trembling Mistress*, 1879). *Banni* echoes the Persian *Saut al-Mubarak*, with treatments of *sur* and *tal*, but these are relatively brief from a theoretical perspective: the primary interest of the work is to document the musical activities of the Matia Burj court, especially lyrical compositions, directions and plots for performances, and a detailed commentary on the musical education of Wajid Ali's court women.

Max Katz's analysis of Kaukab's own treatment of music, the *Jauhar-i Musiqi*, indicates a similar intention to organize and clarify Hindustani music theory. However, Kaukab was writing in the early twentieth century, from a very different social position: in particular, his work was a statement of Muslim *ustadi* scholarship. His brother Karamatullah had attempted to share his own book, the *Israr-i Karamat urf Naghmat-i Nia'mat* (*The Secrets of Miracles* (*/Karamatullah*), Or, *The Melodies of Beneficence* (*/Niamatullah*), 1908) with the Hindu reformer V.N. Bhatkhande. Bhatkhande dismissed this work and its author, an "ignorant and obstinate" hereditary musician.[20] Kaukab's work was essentially a rejoinder, pointing out the Islamic roots of Hindustani music theory and history, but also the depths of his own knowledge of the intricacies of older Persian and Sanskrit texts. This was very different then from Wajid Ali's approach: the *nawab* took it for granted that there was a substantial corpus of Indo-Persian learning at his disposal, but was frustrated by what he saw as arcane redundancies. In particular, the *nawab* desired a textual formulation for dance and musical theatre that had not been provided in earlier works. In other words, Wajid Ali and Kaukab were conversant with the same epistemological tradition, but the *nawab* was an innovator while Kaukab was a curator.

The influence of Wajid Ali's theoretical writings cannot be qualified without further studies of subsequent treatises, noting where the Nawab was adopted or disregarded. Walker has begun this work in her analysis of prescriptions for dance *gat*s (steps)[21] in five works: *Saut al-Mubarak* (1852-53) and *Bani* (1877) by Wajid Ali, and, written in the interval between them, the *Ma'dan al-musiqi* (*The Mine of Music c*.1858, first published 1925), the *Ghunca-yi Rag* (*Garland of Ragas*, 1862-63), and the *Sarmaya-yi 'Ishrat* (*The Value of Pleasure*, 1875). The fourteen *gat*s in *Saut* have not been identified in any earlier treatise, and it is assumed that Wajid Ali was the first to document, if not personally develop them. These were duplicated in the *Ma'dan* (framed by an additional seven) and the *Ghunca* (under alternative names). Walker found that *Sarmaya* had a different combination of *gat*s: some with similar names to those in Saut, but with different descriptions. Intriguingly, Wajid Ali's last work *Banni* has twenty-one *gat*s, which do not follow his earlier fourteen prescriptions in Saut, and are closer to *Sarmaya*.[22] There are several implications to be drawn from Walker's analysis, but in the current context I will underline three. First, textual prescriptions of dance *gat*s were not part of Mughal musicology prior to Wajid Ali's intervention, but were immediately taken up as a standard subject by later musicologists. Second, Wajid Ali was

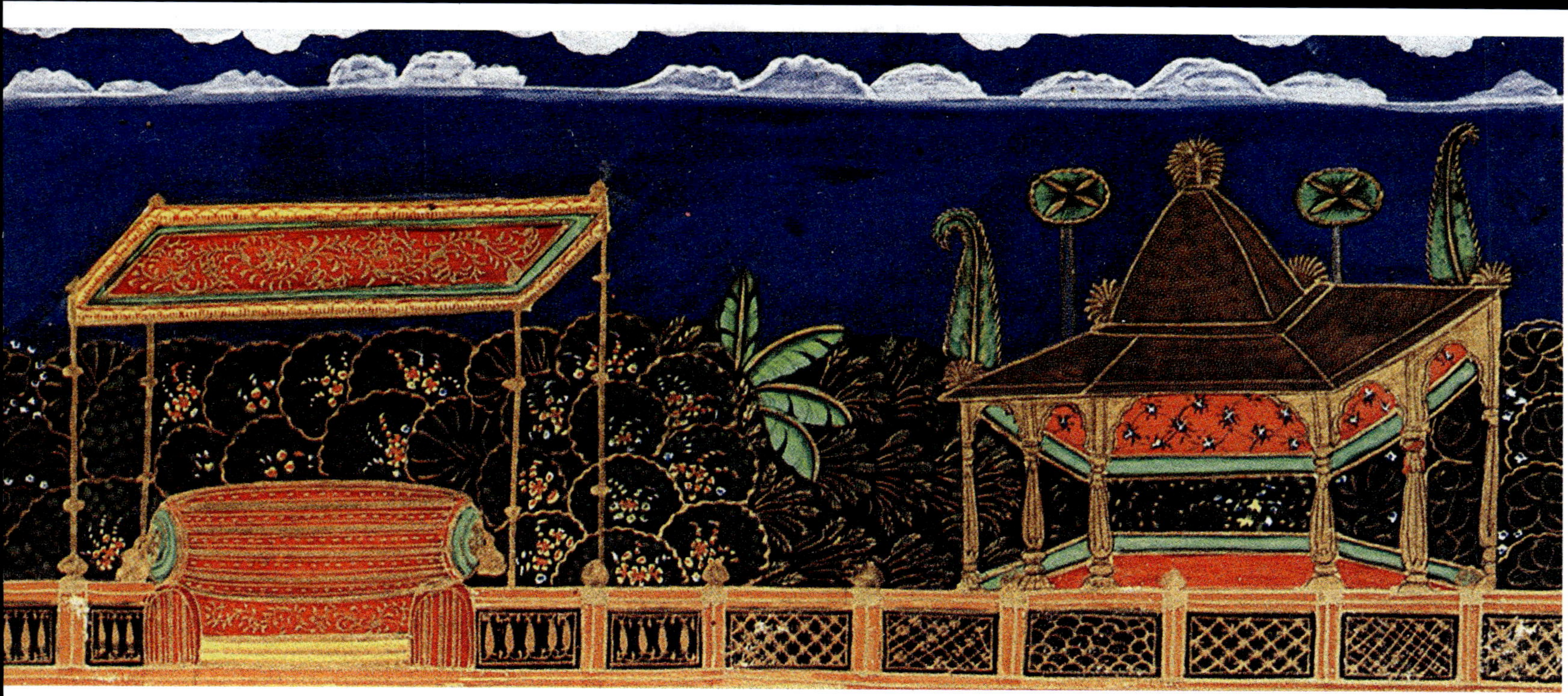

seen as an authority: when Karam Imam developed the *Ma'dan* he turned to both the well-established *Tohfat al-Hind* and the writings of the *nawab*, whom he considered expert. Third, it is apparent from the discrepancies between Wajid Ali's own works that in the twenty-five years between them his thought was evolving, and in dialogue with other connoisseurs (in this case Sadiq Ali Khan, the author of *Sarmaya*). Contrary to Sharar and Kaukab, Wajid Ali was not an ignoramus wholly rejected by "authentic" musicologists. Nor did his cultivation of new directions in music cease abruptly in 1856.

**Tearful Bride or Majestic Elephant?**

Kaukab suggested that the Nawab's musical creations "became popular with the masses with the result that music was cheapened. ... Matters got to the state that if by chance someone listened to pure classical[23] music, he could not appreciate it nor take any interest in it. In fact he often disliked it."[24] According to Kaukab, more elevated forms of music were actively curtailed: "this music had no place in the court and was not appreciated".[25] Kaukab thus drew a contrast between Pyar Khan's music, and the "light, simple, and attractive tunes" favoured by the *nawab*: that is, *thumri* and *ghazal* rather than *dhrupad*. This distinction continues to this day: *thumri* and *ghazal* are considered "semi-classical" and "lighter" vocal genres than *dhrupad* and *khayal*, and have a deeply entrenched association with Wajid Ali, to the extent that he is often mistakenly believed to be the creator of *thumri*.

However, Kaukab evidently did not know about, or chose to ignore, the full range of the *nawab*'s compositions. In his testimonial he identified Wajid Ali by the *takhallus* "Kadar Piya".[26] In fact Wajid Ali did not use this pen name, and consistently wrote as Akhtar, Akhtar Piya, or Akhtar. Kaukab was evidently unfamiliar with the writings he condemned as "cheap". Otherwise, he would have noted the scope of genres that interested Wajid Ali.

*Naju* (compiled 1868) is an anthology of the *nawab*'s lyrics along with those by his senior queen and *nikah* wife, Khas Mahal, who composed extensively under the *takhallus 'alam*. In his introduction, Wajid Ali noted that though he normally wrote as Akhtar he used an alternative (and he thought better suited) spelling, Akhtar, for lyrics in Sanskrit, Hindavi, or Brajbhasha.[27] The compositions are arranged around fifteen genres: songs of praise; *dhrupad; sadra; sargam; caturanga; hori; khayal; tarana; pata; thumri; cacar; savan; dadra; theka* and *dohra*.

Sure enough, *thumri* features prominently, with 117 compositions. However, Wajid Ali was not the principal lyricist. He gave his *takhallus* to thirty-one *thumri*s in this collection (further identified as coming "from the author", *min mussannif*), five belong to five additional writers,[28] while the majority – eighty-one lyrics – are by Khas Mahal. Since each genre section is subdivided by *ragini* it is also clear that Khas Mahal wrote for a larger range of *ragini*s: many subdivisions contain only her lyrics. When Wajid Ali wrote a *thumri* for a *ragini*, such as *Khamach*, he placed his lyrics first: his take precedence before Khas Mahal in each section, but are drowned out by the number of her compositions. Wajid Ali's *thumri*s predominate in

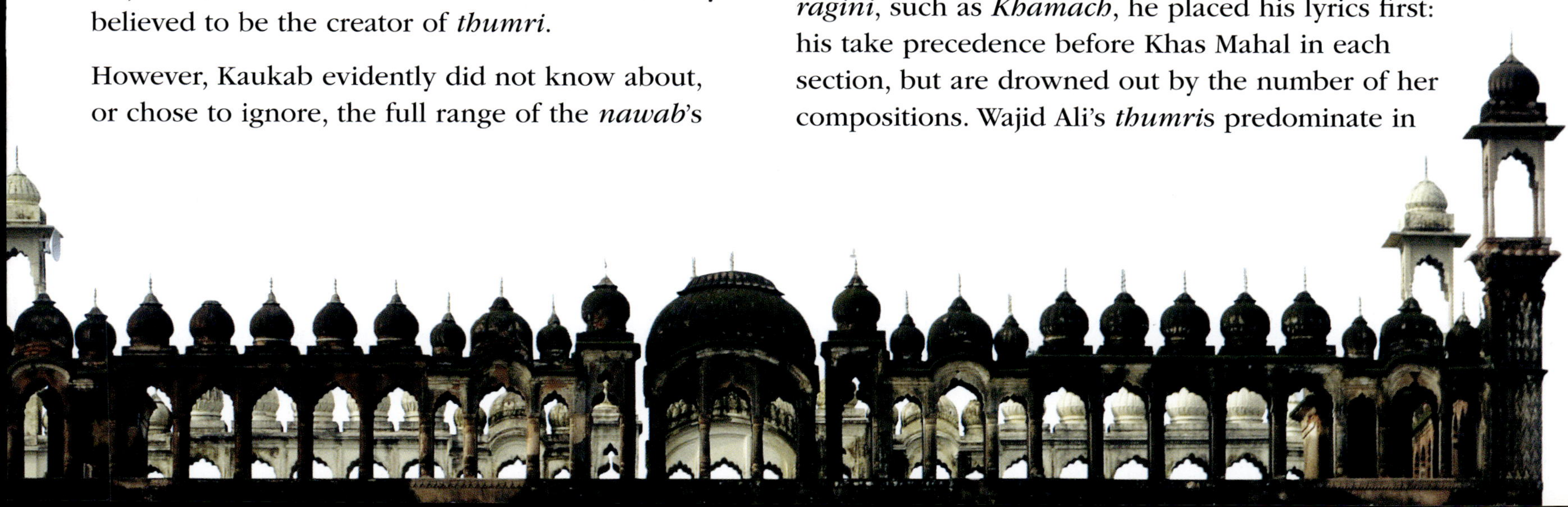

the section dedicated not to a *ragini* but to *rahas*.[29] That the queen wrote more than double the number of *thumri* lyrics than the *nawab* indicates that his fame as the pioneer of the genre demands further qualification, as does the importance of women in the history of music.

While some of the genre chapters are quite thin, *dhrupad* is very well represented with sixty-seven lyrics, of which twenty-four are by Wajid Ali himself, thirty-five by Khas Mahal, one that they wrote together,[30] and one each by Nayak Bakhsu, Nayak Gopal, Nayak Biju, Tansen, and Pyar Khan. The appearance of Pyar Khan is especially striking, given that Kaukab claimed that Pyar was unappreciated in court.[31] In their *dhrupads*, the royal couple used innovative language to explore traditional subjects. Khas Mahal, for instance, wrote several lyrics to the God Rama (King of Ayodhya, so of special relevance to the royal family of Awadh) which fused registers of Hindu imagery with local Islamicate references: "Raja Rama, flawless Hindu Lord and Sultan! ...".[32] Wajid Ali wrote a *dhrupad* in his own honour, set in *ragini* Sultani, his own invention (*ijad-i musannif*). When sung in *cautal*, the song was apparently intended as a declaration of his creative genius and majesty:

**Astai**

*'alam-panah shah akhtar sultan-i 'alam thik kahayo*

**Antara**

*jin tujhe sultan*
*jano sar bhed tir vahi*
*mano gaj turang in'am payo*

Rightly called Protector of the Universe, Shah,
Akhtar, Sultan of the Universe!
He who is "Sultan" to you is
Like multitudes of arrows from one bow
Like receiving honours of elephants and horses.[33]

Wajid Ali's experimentation with *dhrupad* and his composing on the subject of his own majesty are in contrast to the popular image of the effeminate *nawab*, famous for a *thumri* in which he took on the persona of a tearful bride.

Aside from the lyric collections, there is extensive evidence of *dhrupad* at Matia Burj. Wajid Ali continued the musical instruction of court women from Lucknow's *parikhana* in Calcutta, organized into "assemblies" (*jalsa*). Many of these women were associated with his novel musical theatricals, but several others were given training in established genres, including *dhrupad*. Wajid Ali noted that the women of the Choti Jalsa (Small Assembly) were dismally untalented, but nonetheless he deigned to teach them a few of his own *dhrupad* compositions.[34] Given that today *dhrupad* is considered an extremely complex, and primarily masculine art-form, this in itself seems extraordinary. While this *jalsa* was a disappointment, Wajid Ali delightedly reported that other assemblies, such as the Nur Manzil (House of Light), were extremely skilled (*kritiyan*) in *dhrupad* and made their audiences weep with pleasure.[35] These women required instruction, and many of the male musicians in court specialized in *dhrupad*: they included Hindustani *ustads* and their Bengali disciples who recognized Matia Burj as a centre of traditional training as well as innovative entertainments.

While Sharar presented a vibrant account of Lucknow, we need to read his tales of court culture with a grain of salt. In the case of music, Sharar's ideas about Wajid Ali Shah's decadent tastes and neglect of serious scholarship have had a profound effect on how the Nawab has been remembered. However, the journalist's source was not wholly reliable. Kaukab was a remarkable musician with superb family credentials, and also an accomplished intellectual. However, his judgement about Wajid Ali Shah was misleading: the *nawab* did not neglect musicological literature or "elevated" genres such as *dhrupad*, but rather wrote, published, and taught his own contributions to these fields in his personal music school. While he certainly enjoyed *thumri*, particularly in its connection to musical theatre (*rahas*), this was hardly his only investment, and his wife composed far more lyrics than he did. Kaukab thus presented a one-dimensional vision of the *nawab*, but also crafted the musical legacy of Matia Burj to suit the demands and struggles he faced as a professional *ustad* in the early twentieth century. By lamenting Wajid Ali's "cheapening" forays into music, and simultaneously extolling the virtues of the "neglected" Pyar Khan and Basat Khan, he positioned himself as the custodian of a "superior kind" (*a'la qism*) of music at a time when Muslim musicians were losing ground in public debates about India's musical heritage. The *nawab*'s own writings from Matia Burj indicate a breadth of interests and skills far beyond Kaukab's characterization, a creative period of evolution and development that cannot be seen as pertaining to an "old" or "lost" culture.

**Notes**

1 Kaukab Qadr Sajjad Ali Mirza, 1995, *Vajid 'Ali Shah ki adabi aur saqafati khidmat, Taraqqi-yi Urdu Biyuro*, New Delhi; Masud Hasan Rizvi, 1977, *Sultan-i 'alam Wajid 'Ala Shah: ek tarikhi muraqqa*, Lucknow: All India Mir Academy.

2 Abdul Halim Sharar, 1971, *Hindustan mein mashraqi tamaddun ka akhiri namunah: yan'i guzashtah-yi Lakhna'u*, New Delhi: Maktabah-yi Jamiah; English tr.,

1975, *Lucknow: The Last Phase of an Oriental Culture*, by E.S. Harcourt and Fakhir Hussain, London: Paul Elek.

3 C.M. Naim, 2012, "Interrogating 'The East,' 'Culture,' and 'Loss,' in Abdul Halim Sharar's Guzashta Lakhna'u," in A. Patel and K. Leonard, *Indo-Muslim Cultures in Transition*, Leiden: Brill, p. 189.

4 Sharar, *Lucknow*, p. 74.

5 Naim, 'Interrogating', p. 193; Sharar, *Lucknow*, p. 193.

6 Sharar, *Lucknow*, p. 193; cf. p. 47.

7 Mirza Jafar Hussain, 1981, *Qadim Lakhna'u ki akhiri bahar*, New Delhi: Taraqqi-yi Urdu Biyuro.

8 Naim, 'Interrogating', p. 203.

9 Sharar, *Lucknow*, p. 137.

10 Ibid., pp. 137-38.

11 Ibid., p. 138.

12 Max Katz, 2017, *Lineage of Loss: Counternarratives of North Indian Music*, Middletown: Wesleyan University Press, pp. 60-61.

13 Wajid Ali Shah, *c.*1852, *Saut al-Mubarak*, unpublished MS, The British Library, London, 14835.e.1 p. 5; see Rizvi, *Sultan*, pp. 161-63.

14 Kippen notes that Wajid Ali's treatment of *tala* is quite distinctive: the *nawab* mixed old and new terms from Persian and Sanskrit, omitted "uncommon" *tala*s that he thought redundant, and also did not provide the *theka*s for *tala*s he had not personally practised. See James Kippen, 2012, "Eighteenth and Nineteenth Century Sources on Rhythm and Drumming in North India: Mapping the Rhythmic Revolution", unpublished working paper, p. 25.

15 From the Urdu translation of the Persian original, Rizvi, *Sultan*, p. 162.

16 Rosie Llewellyn-Jones, 2014, *The Last King in India: Wajid Ali Shah*, London: C. Hurst, pp. 261-63.

17 Wajid Ali Shah, 1877, *Banni*, Calcutta: Matba'-i Sultani, p. 243.

18 Wajid Ali Shah, 1869, *Naju*, Calcutta: Matba'-i Sultani.

19 Wajid Ali Shah, 1873, *Dulhan*, Calcutta: Matba'-i Sultani.

20 Cited in Janaki Bakhle, 2005, *Two Men and Music: Nationalism in the Making of an Indian Classical Tradition*, New York: Oxford University Press, pp. 109-12.

21 The *gat* is the building block of extended dance sequences, known in contemporary performance as *nikas* or *bhav*. See, Margaret E. Walker, 2014, "The 'Nautch' Reclaimed: Women's Performance Practice in Nineteenth-Century North India", *South Asia: Journal of South Asian Studies*, 37: 8.

22 Ibid., pp. 9-14.

23 "Pure classical" is Harcourt and Hussain's translation; the original reads *a'la qism*, "superior order" of music.

24 Sharar, *Lucknow*, p. 137.

25 Ibid., p. 138.

26 Ibid., p. 137.

27 Shah, *Naju*, pp. 2-3.

28 Identified by *takhallus* as Nasr, Jalal, Nizami, Rang and Hans Malha.

29 Shah, *Naju*, pp. 199ff.

30 Ibid., pp. 60-61.

31 Ibid., pp. 25-26; see also a *sadra* by Pyar Khan, pp. 72-73.

32 *Raja Rama niranjana hindu pati saltan* ... Shah, *Naju*, p. 29, cf. 48-49.

33 Shah, *Naju*, pp. 44-45.

34 Shah, *Bani*, pp. 318-19.

35 Ibid., p. 319.

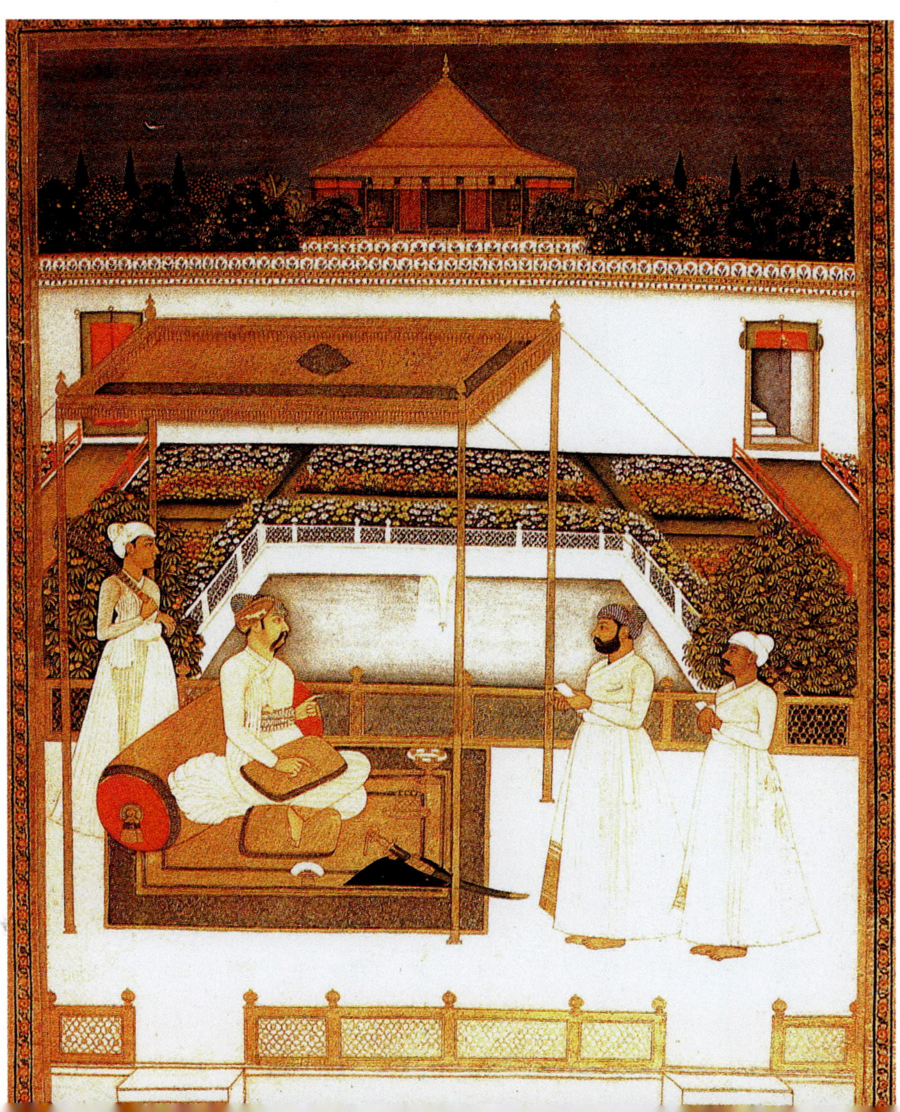

*Court scene, Awadh, 19th century*

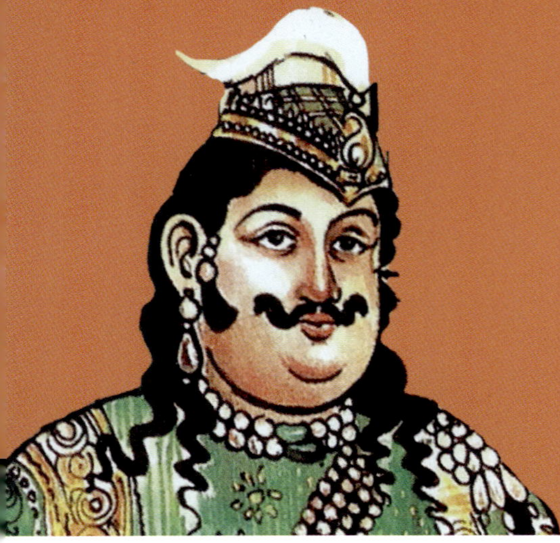

# Exploring Nawab Wajid Ali's Flourishes of Beauty

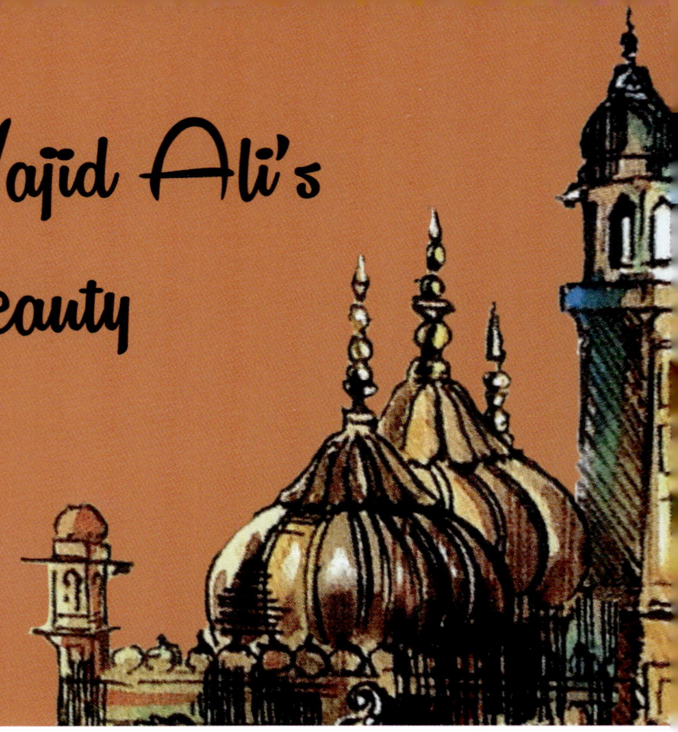

**Sunil Sunkara**

The notion of beauty and the factors that create it are both fluid and subtle. The *Natyashastra* talks of *rechaks* that add beauty to every movement. While Bharata leaves the exploration of *rechaks* to the creativity and virtuosity of the performer, he mentions that the subtle *rechak* is the distinguishing factor between physical exercise and graceful dance. Approximately fifteen centuries later, Rana Kumbharaja in his *Nrityaratnakosha* talks of *anukaran* (imitation) of nature in order to create graceful beauty in dance. While beauty is a matter of perception, these perceptions get crystallized over a period of time as generation after generation subscribe to the same ideal. When we look at the creative arts of Awadh, the one person who has been directly or indirectly responsible in setting those ideals of beauty is Nawab Wajid Ali Shah. By the eighteenth-century music and dance were primarily sustained though patronization by the royal courts. Art influences art and the presence of a competitive atmosphere created in the *darbaar* lead to the development of intricacy in narratives of both rhythm and prose. Nawab Wajid Ali's aesthetics were a touchstone for beauty that resulted in creating the hallmark *nazaakat* and *nafaasat* (spotless and delicate beauty), which resonates within the music and dance of Awadh.

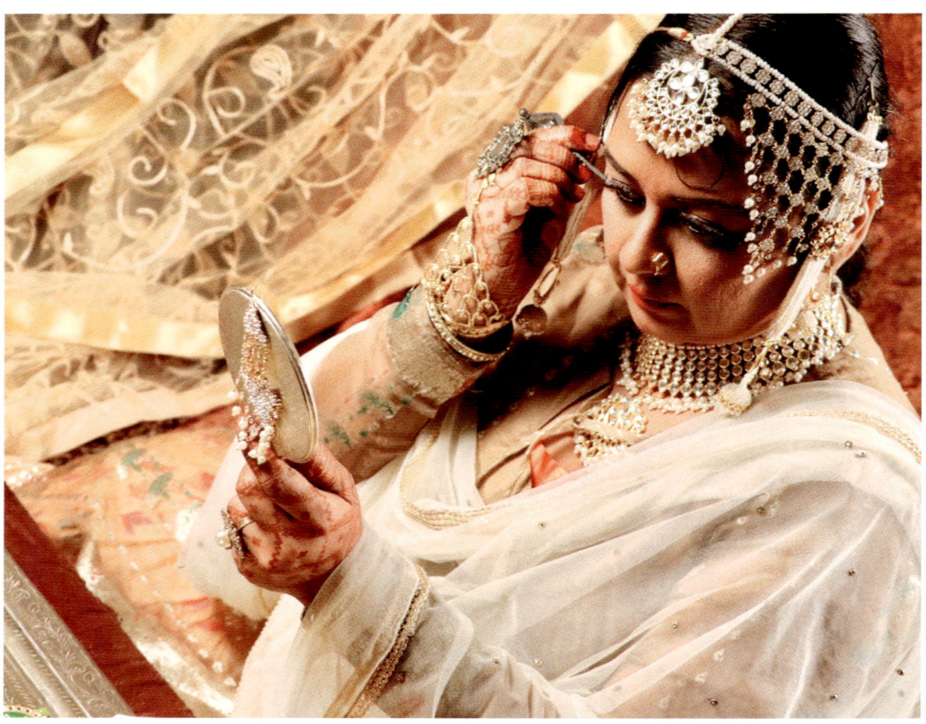

*Image 1: Pari's Shringaar, Dancer: Paullumi B. Mukheerjee, PC: Karan Kishan Photography, St. Andrews Centre for Philosophy and Performing Art, Mumbai*

The Nawab's approach can be analysed through the fourfold principles of *abhinaya-aangik* (through a study of *rahas* movements), *vaachik* (through a study of scripts and compositions written by him), *aharya* (the costumes of his *darbaar*) and finally his fine-tuned appreciation of *sattva*.

*chalo chalo sakhi ab rahas kare,*
*akhtarpiya ke mann ko rijhaye ...*

Come dear friend, lets begin the dance of love,
Let's make Akhtarpiya (Nawab) rejoice in its glow. ...

The above couplet, gives a direct insight into Wajid Ali's aesthetic sense. The word *rijhana* means enticement. Through poetry and dance, Wajid Ali searched for an enticement of the mind, body and soul, which in other words is an immersion in *rasa*. He used himself as the sounding board for all the maestros and dancers in his court, almost like a litmus test. If a composition or a dance was able to bring out those emotions in his own highly cultured and intelligent persona, it passed the touchstone for beauty. This is how his patronage become crucial for the evolution and development of the *bandish ki thumri* as well as

Lakhnavi *andaaz* of Kathak in the Lucknow court. It is during Wajid Ali's time that beauty in dance came to be associated with subtle flourishes such as the raising of an eyebrow, the delicate movement of a wrist, expansion and contraction of the torso and subtle use of the pupils. It was these flourishes of beauty that took the viewer on the journey from *wah, kya baat hai!* (voluntary applause) to *'aaah, kya baat hai!'* (involuntary appreciation).

In the book *Banni* written by Wajid Ali Shah, he describes and illustrates various poses to be used for the *rahas*, which loosely means *raas* or the dance of *shringaar*. In the book he says that these *rahas* have been developed by him based on his understanding from the maestros or *ustads*. He also goes on to explain *rahas vistrit* through a dance ballet, *Kissa Radha Kanhaiya Ka*. The book *Banni* has been written during the Nawab's confinement by the British at Matia Burj in Bengal, post-1857 and has been translated from original Farsi to Hindi by Roshan Taqi.

Though Wajid Ali Shah does not directly refer to Lucknow's Kathak or the Maharaj dynasty in his book, the depiction of *rahas* clearly has a connection to the Lucknow Gharana *parampara*.

*Guzashta-i-Lucknau* by Abdul Halim Shara mentions the names of Durga Prasad and Thakur Prasad, identified as one Prakash's sons, and it is the first place that mentions that Thakur taught Wajid Ali Shah to dance. The historical connections placing Thakur Prasad in the court of Wajid Ali, further supports the hypothesis that the *rahas* would be based on the prevalent Kathak poses, footwork patterns and stances developed in the court. This can be seen from the only available painting of Thakur Prasad where his costume and stance both show a remarkable similarity to the *rahas* postures illustrated by Wajid Ali. At the same time one has to keep in mind that dance in the court did not necessarily mean to imply a dancer wearing *ghungroos* on his feet. Just the indication of an emotion through a beautiful movement of the body would be called as a dance. One has to observe the populace of Lucknow, who even today display a certain lyricism of movement in their daily actions. Thus when we think of Thakur Prasad teaching Wajid Ali dance, one must not imagine a proscenium Kathak dancer wearing *ghungroos* presenting a Kathak repertoire as seen today. We can justify that statement by imagining how the grace of poetry could be translated into subtle movement vocabulary of dance, which could then possibly go on to become a part of everyday expression which has come to be called the Lakhnavi *adab*.

In the chapter on *rahas*, Wajid Ali describes a number of *gats*. *Gat* is derived from the word *gati* and is used to describe a movement. But Wajid Ali's elaboration leads us to use the term *gat* as "coming into a unique position". He describes sixteen Kathak *gats* and five Keherva *gats*.

*First Salaami Gat (Pehli Salaami Gat)*
The dancer should stand facing towards the audience and all the fingers must be joined with the first finger of the right hand must be on the forehead, thumb must be separate. Left hand in a tight fist must be on the waist in the shape of a half-moon till the shoulder. Then, dance should be done in front of the audience with right profile towards the audience. We observe a natural separation of the thumb from the remaining fingers. This enables movement of the wrist, one of the factors responsible for creating beauty in dance movements, and an integral part of Kathak training today.

*Fourth Fariyaad Gat (Chauthi Fariyaad Gat)*
Both hands should be stretched sideways fully, face should be towards the audience and while going back left hand should be towards the audience.

*Sixth Naaz Gat (Chati Naaz Gat)*
While joining the fingers of the right hand, the middle finger should be kept on the chin in such a manner that palm is visible to the audience. Left hand should be according to the *moaddab gat*. While going back, right profile should be towards the audience.

*Seventh Gamza Gat (Saatvi Gamaza Gat)*
Keep the right hand in a fist on the chest and the left hand similar to the *naaz gat*. While beginning the dance, first show your right profile to the audience.

*Ninth Crown Gat (Nauva Mukut Gat)*
'The fingers of both the hands must be criss-crossed into each other's crevices. Both the elbows till the shoulders should be in the shape of a full moon and hands must be four fingers above the head. While going back, the poses should be according to previous *gats*.' Here we see an instance of how Wajid Ali's aesthetic made its way into popular culture in the twenty-first century. Meena Kumari in the iconic movie *Pakeezah* depicts the *mukut gat* in the *ghazal* '*chalte chalte yuh hi koi*' choreographed by Pt Lacchu Maharaj.

*Tenth Lucknowi Ghunghat Gat*
Stretch the *ghoonghat* through the left hand towards the bellybutton in such a manner that half the right face gets covered by *ghoonghat*. Right hand should be on right head with palm facing outside. While going back, the poses should be according to previous *gats*.

No illustration was provided by Wajid Ali for this *gat*. This could be due to the very *lokadharmi* nature of this movement, as it reflects the natural way to hold the veil.

While studying the *rahas* depictions by Wajid Ali, one realizes that an illustration captures a moment in time, that is symbolic of both oral traditions and history, while a *gharana* (school of thought), captures an essence in real time. In the introduction to the *gats*, Wajid Ali mentions that those who are training in dance under him at Matia Burj are getting trained in the very same *gats* described by him in *Banni*, and due to his innate wish of making them available to all dance lovers, he has worked on the documentation of the *gats* in his book. This thus shows us another aspect of the Nawab, that of the mentor. His approach is reflective of a person who has the real desire to influence and propagate the art, and not just that of an entitled patron, one just enjoying the art for his pleasure. This truly sets apart Nawab Wajid Ali and is a testament to his work being relevant even today.

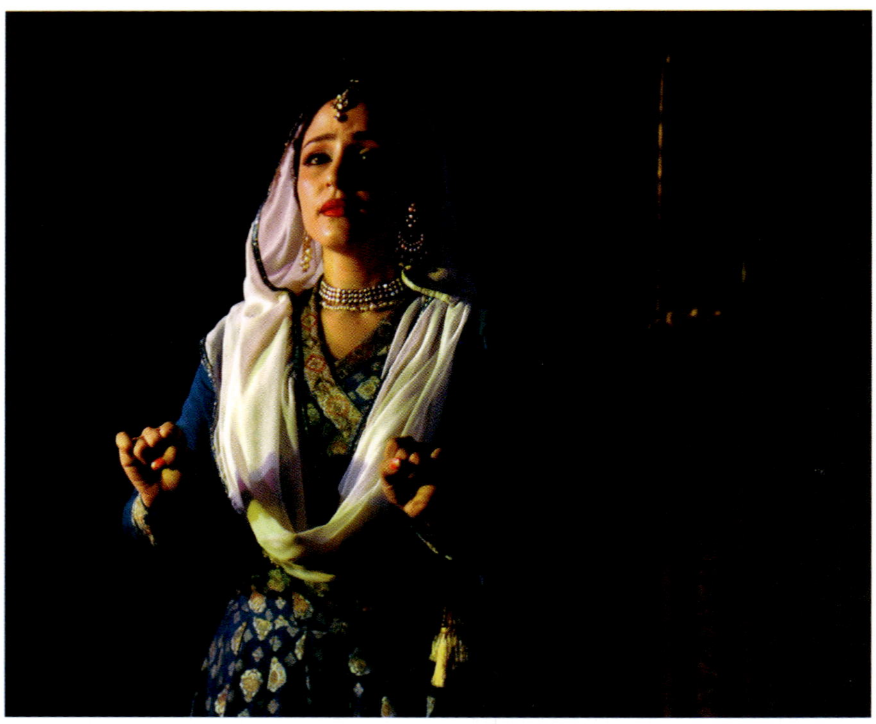

*Image 2: Dancer depicting lovelorn Nayika, Dancer: Natalia Hildner, PC: Alpika, Lucknow*

A single beautiful thought (*vikaar*) in the formless mind translates into spontaneity of *sattva* when that thought completes a cycle, beginning from intangible expression, climaxing in the tangible expression of the written word. This can again journey back to the intangible through an abstract expression through the medium of the body. Wajid Ali through his poems gives life to those intangible impressions that are the true life force within delicate movements, beautiful words and subtle beauty.

The books written by Wajid Ali on poetry and art carry titles like *Banni*, *Naajo* and *Saut ul Mubarak* that signify a bride, heralding that the reader would be stepping into a world of romanticism. In his book *Naajo*, Wajid Ali documents compositions written by him that cover the wide range of *dhrupad, sadra, sargam, chaturang, hori, khayal, tarana, sindhi geet, thumri, hori, saavan, dadra* and *dohas*. While he covers a wide range of topics, in the *nayika*-based compositions he favours the lovelorn heroine, the *proshitpatika*, one whose love has travelled to a distant land, or *virahotkantita*, one separated from her lover for a long period. A few lines of his were made popular through the Satyajit Ray classic *Shatranj ke khiladi*:

*tadap tadap sagari raina gujari, kaun desh gayo saavariya? ubal gayi akhiya matwari, aur tarak tarak gayi chunariya. tumhare ghodan mere dwar se jo nikle, sudhi bool gayi mein baawariya, araja kari sapne mein 'akhtar', base tumhari paturiya.*

I spent each moment of the night in terrible angst, where have you disappeared? My eyes have boiled over with tears, in hot rivulets that have left their mark on my veil. When I heard your horses leave my doorstep, I lost control of my senses. All I wish for in dream and when awake, is to be one with Akhtar.

The word Akhtar, Wajid Ali's pseudonym, takes on a number of roles in the compositions. While Akhtar is the divine lord for whom Wajid yearns, at the same time Akhtar is also the lover that the heroine longs for. A two-line *hori* written by Wajid Ali beautifully puts across this thread of thought,

*doobte dil ke paar lagaiya, 'akhtar' sai naav khivaiya*

Akhtar is the oarsman who rescues my drowning heart.

A *thumri* that paints the typical imagery of the *proshitpatika*

*aajahu na aaaye saiyya, kaise samjhau jiyara un bina? viraha vyathaki main maari marat ho, sun ae sakhi ri, dagmag parat ki dagmag pair, ginat tare saari rain beeti.*

He hasn't returned yet, how do I make my heart understand? The angst of separation is slowly killing me, Oh *sakhi*! My feet have lost control of direction, all I do is spend the night counting stars.

In contrast to the previous typical portrayal, Wajid Ali creates an out of the box imagery in this next *thumri*, which resonates with the Ganga–Jamuni *tehzeeb* in his court,

*bhor bhaye nahi aaye baalam, nisa uthat uthat jiya haar gayo trishool se nainan jaay ladho, dujhe hool se seenan maar gayo, gaayan kandarbha ki batiya karo, ramayan se taan ko tool, 'akhtar' dhun ko uchaar gayo.*

The sun rose, but her lover did not return. Every dawn further waning her enthusiasm. My eyes kept fighting with all kinds of fear, fear that made my heart sink I search for "Akhtar" who suddenly disappeared after singing a tune which was set to a metre as beautiful as the *Ramayana*, in a voice as beautiful as the celestial *gandharvas*.

We see shades of *sufi* love in a number of compositions by Wajid Ali. A recurring motif in *sufi shringaar* is the *dagar* or the road upon which the *nayika* interacts with the divine lover. Wajid Ali writes,

*saiyya aavan ki bhanak suni main, rahi dagariya taak ve, palkan se main dagar buharoon, yahi hamari aas ve.*

Getting a slight indication that he would be arriving soon, I started gazing upon the road. All I wish for is that my eyelashes sweep the path, preparing it for his arrival.

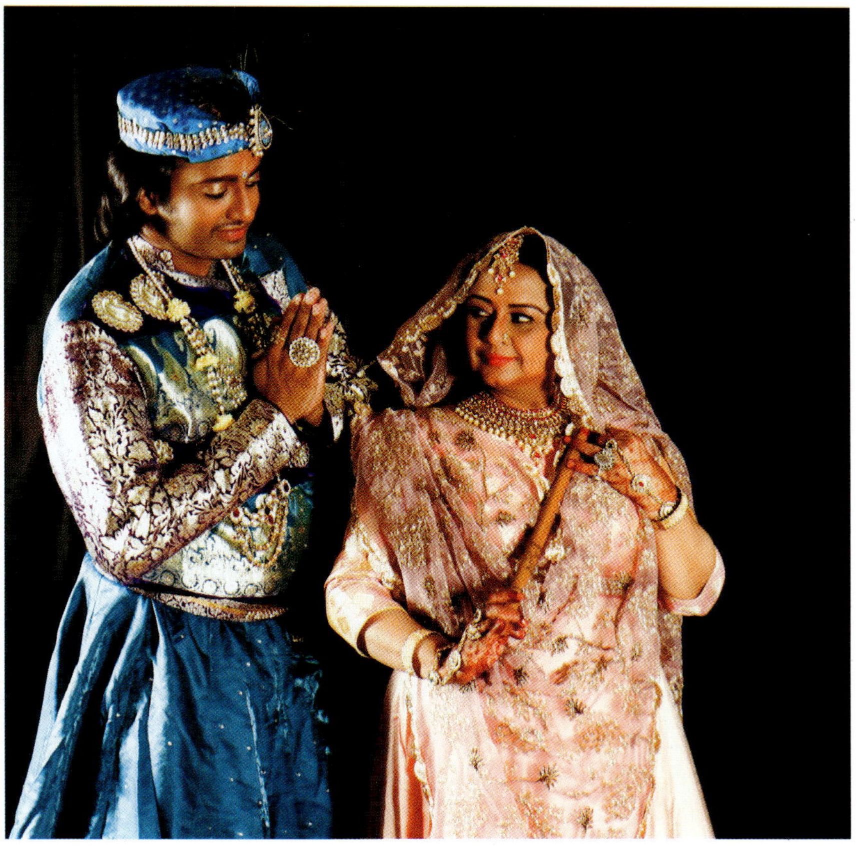

*Image 3: Krishna Begging Paniharin for His Flute, Dancers: Sunil Sunkara and Paullumi B. Mukheerjee, PC: Karan Kishan Photography, St Andrews Centre for Philosophy and Performing Art, Mumbai*

We see an inspiration taken from Mirabai in this next composition, that again resonates with the *sufi* ethos of yearning:

*ud jaa re kaaga, saiyya kab aavenge, ud ud kaaga sagun bicharo, saiyya ke darsan kab paavenge.*

Wajid Ali asks the *kaaga* (bird) to fly away and ask the world, when would the divine lover return to give him *darshan*?

The yearning of a *nayika* often intensifies in the monsoon. Wajid Ali depicts such an imagery in the following *saavan*, where we see how mating and separation in the surrounding nature makes the heroine contemplate upon her own condition.

*yah dukh saha na jaaye, bijali chamaki jiyara laraje Saapin choda saap ka sangh, nadiyan chodi re karar Saiyya ne choda mara jobanva*

I cant bear this pain. The lightening rends apart my heart. The mating snakes have gone apart, The river has abandoned the shore just like my lover has left me. ...

Wajid Ali's search continued as he explored the arts, sometimes in search of solace, sometimes as a distraction, but mostly to connect with that greater energy that one finds distilled into all great art. Four lines of a *dadra* left by him connect the *proshitpatika*'s friend – the cuckoo (*koyal*), the fish emblem of the Awadh state (the *machali*) and the despondency in the Nawab as "Akhtar" left his beloved city for Matia Burj in 1857.

*baag suna re koyal bina*
the garden lies vacant, bereft of the call of the cuckoo

*taal suna re machali bina*
the pond lies vacant, bereft of the playful fish

*baat suna re batohi bina*
the road lies vacant, bereft of the seeker

*seja suna re baalam bina*
the bed lies vacant, bereft of the divine lover.

A popular composition written by Wajid Ali, it shows how he modelled himself and his *paris* (fairies) after Krishna and his *gopis*. By the Ritikaal Krishna had become a courtly character as seen in a number of poetic as well as painted depictions. Wajid a seeker of beauty, found resonance within this ethos of beauty leading to divinity.

*mohan rasiya aaye bagiya,*
*chuma rahe ras kali kali ri*
*koi kali hari naam pukare,*
*koi kali kahe ali ali ri*

Mohan, the seeker of pleasure, entered the garden,
like a bee drinking nectar from various flowers,
Some flowers call out the name "Hari",
while some call out the name "Ali".

In the above composition he paints a parallel picture between Hari's love sports and Ali's (his own) opulent harem. In some poems he himself becomes Krishna as evident in the line,

*vrindavan chali radha pyari,*
*"akhtar" phod do ke mataki*

Look, Radha is on her way to Vrindavana,
Akhtar, it's time to break her pitcher.

At the same time, he also writes poetry where he identifies himself as "Radha", showing how he himself was in search of that divine pleasure

*jugal kishore bansuri bajavat,*
*chado kunjan aur galiyan,*
*"akhtar" radha ko sangh chalo mathura,*
*vana vija karate rangaraliya.*

A young Krishna plays the flute,
come let us abandon the lanes of Vrindavana
Akhtar sojourns with Radha,
to enjoy revelries in the forest of Mathura.

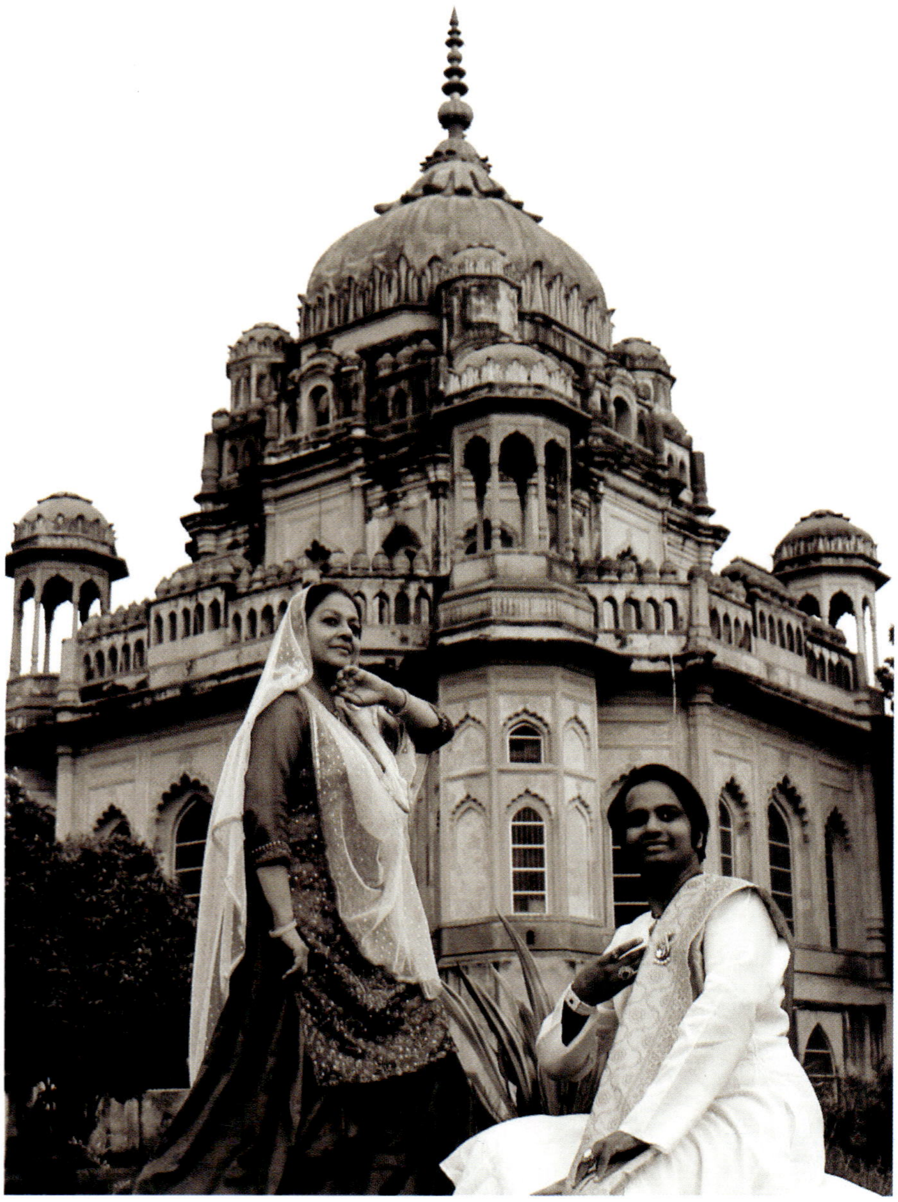

Image 4: Court Dancers, Dancers: Renu Sharma and Sunil Sunkara, PC: Amit Trigunayat, Lucknow

In the imageries created by Wajid Ali through his poems as well as opulent productions of *rahas*, we see a coming to life of the beautiful miniature paintings we associate with the medieval period, most strikingly in the costumes worn by his *paris*. In the book *Banni*, he describes the *poshak* (suitable attire) to be worn by the *pari* to consist of four main components: *karchobi dupatta* (embroidered veil), *jamaye husn purjar* (diaphanous bodice with a voluminous frock), *payjama purjar* (translucent pants) and *jumala zevar* (ornaments). His emphasis on *purjari* or translucent clothing reminds one of the dancers depicted in miniatures wearing almost transparent outfits, which reveal the beautiful geometries created by the body of the dancer.

By surrounding himself with the *paris* with both their physical beauty as well as creative stimuli, Wajid Ali developed an outlook of finding beauty within unlikely situations. An often repeated story highlights this aesthetic of Wajid Ali. Once a *pari* let slip from her hands the cord that was being pulled by her to secure a chandelier in place. This chandelier was one of the Nawab's favourites and had been carefully transported from Lucknow to Matia Burj. As the chandelier came crashing to the ground, hearing the sound of the breaking glass, all Wajid Ali said was, *wah!, kya khanak hai*. Instead of fretting over the loss of the chandelier, his instant reaction was to appreciate the reverberation of breaking glass. Only a person devoted to appreciating beauty in every moment would give such an involuntary response!

For Wajid and his fairies, their quest for beauty was an auspicious (*mubarak*) journey, as seen in the poem *Jaan-e-alam*, that Satyajit Ray used effectively in his introduction of actor Amjad Khan as Wajid Ali Shah engrossed in the *jogia jashn*.

*jaan-e-alam rahas*
*mubarak jug jug*
*jiyo sadaa birajo,*
*"akhtar" sangh sakhi sahas mubarak*

The light of the world dances the auspicious
*rahas*, "Akhtar" and his fairies enjoy this dance
for a long time to come.

*Inder Sabha* was a significant coming together of Persian tastes with Hindu mythology which resonated with Parsi theatre as well as early films. Wajid Ali's *rahas* plays further went on to inspire popular folk culture and even today in Chhattisgarh and Awadh, the term *rahas* is used to denote folk theatre, where along with the *vidushak* and *sutradhar*, the *pari* has become a mainstream character who appears in various scenes of the play.

*Rahas*, an extension of the word *raas*, was truly brought to life in Wajid Ali's *Rahas Vistrut* that coalesced the various elements of his aesthetics under his play *Kissa Radha Kanhaiya Ka*. Set in the appealing play within a play format, the central character is a *jogan* Sehra who is in sorrow that she has been unable to see the dance of Radha and Kanhaiyya for twenty-four years. Sehra is taken to Wajid's fairies who decide to fulfil her request by immediately staging the dance drama of Radha-Kanhaiya which begins with a *jhoola, hindola jhoole shyama shyam*.

At Wajid Ali's birth it was prophesized that he would become a *jogi*. In order to avoid that, seers advised that he should lead the life of a *jogi* for one day every year on his birthday. This in Wajid Ali's later years manifested as the *jogia jashn* where he and his *pari*s would adorn themselves as *jogi*s. Legend has it that Wajid Ali would smear himself with ash made from burning pearls, an opulence that wouldn't suit any other *jogi* but "Akhtar". In the *jogia jashn* Wajid Ali's chief *begum*s dressed up as *jogan*s, and one could imagine that Wajid Ali fashioned his Sehra emulating the *jogan* costume worn by his *begums*.

As the *kissa* proceeds we see the familiar plot of Radha being angry with Krishna's mischiefs, which in reality resonates with Wajid often having to placate his various favourite *begums*. Wajid Ali writes the following lines for Kanhaiya:

*meri maharani radha rani,*
*kya mose kuch chuka padi,*
*meri rani "akhtar" kadar na jaani*

My queen Radha, did I really make a mistake?
Why does my queen not realize the worth of the
star (Akhtar) she has?

*radhaji mohase bolo kyun na re?*
*kya mose kuch chukka padi meri rani,*
*hasa-hasa ghunghat kholo kyun na re?*

Why doesn't Radha speak to me? Did I make a
mistake my queen? Why does your smiling face
not look out from under your veil?

Radha then asks Krishna to play his flute to appease her, but at this time Krishna realizes that his flute has gone missing. Thus begins the central section of the play, with Krishna searching for his flute. Here Wajid Ali effectively uses the *vidushak* (jester) to create levity through the character Ramchera, who shadows Krishna in his search for the missing flute. Each time Kanhaiya calls out "Has anyone seen my *murali* (flute)?" Ramchera replaces the word *murali* with words like *murgi* (cock), *bhaisa* (bull), etc. *Hasya* is an important aesthetic in making an audience open up to a story and Wajid Ali effectively uses this aesthetic. Immediately in contrast to this, a traveller tells Krishna that his flute was seen with one of the *panibarin*s (water bearers) at the river front. Thus from the levity of Ramchera we are immediately transported to the beautiful *panibarins*. The *panibarin gat* is popular even today in Kathak, where the beauty of filling the pitcher of water is explored through delicate movements of the wrist, accompanied by breath control and torso movements. Wajid Ali introduces his *panibarin*s singing a beautiful *thumri*,

*sab raah baat mein dhoond phiri, vrindavan*
*mein ho saavariya jangal jangal sunsaan bhayo,*
*sun paayi na kaisi baansuriya pag dharat dharat*
*lat palat gayo, kar pakarat kangan uchaka gayo*
*chal chad de "akhtar" baangariya*

I roamed the lanes of Vrindavana, searching for
you my beloved. Even though the jungle was
silent, I couldn't hear a single strain of your
flute. As I was walking suddenly I looked back,
as someone's hand on my wrist had broken my
bangles! Let go of my little finger oh "Akhtar"!

Krishna offers the *panibarin laddu*s in return for his flute, but she demands that he bring her butter in exchange for his flute. In a loveable turn around, Krishna who usually steals butter, now has to beg butter from a *makhanwali* who is enroute to the city to sell her butter to the Nawab "Akhtar". Thus we now see Wajid introducing his own self into the play through the composition,

*ae deyi mein makhan bechan jaat,*
*na lo kanha tum makhan mora,*
*bechu "akhtar"; haath*

I am on my way to sell butter,
Don't take the butter from me Oh Krishna!
I want to sell it to "Akhtar".

Krishna somehow manages to steal a handful of butter from the *makhanwali* and get his flute back in exchange. The *kissa* concludes with the song,

*bajan laagi shyam ki bansuri re*
*nadiya kinare "akhtar" bansuri bajavat re*

Shyam plays his flute once again at the banks of
the river, the bright star plays the flute.

This poem again connects with the *jogia jashn*, where in conclusion to the day-long celebrations, on the banks of the Gomti, in the presence of his close companions, the Nawab would pretend to be Kanhaiyaa.

Thus through his journey of *raha*s with his literary brides *Banni* and *Naajo* and a number of other memorable characters, the Nawab takes the reader into a world of his subtle aesthetic of metaphors and memories. Though history tends to focus on Wajid Ali's life and associated politics, if one views him through the lens of an artist, one can notice the flourishes of beauty that have left golden imprints on the fabric of our cultural quilt.


### Acknowledgements

I thank Renu Sharma, a Kathak exponent who carries the essence of Lucknow in her work, for her guidance and teachings over the years in enabling me to understand Wajid Ali's work and well as her inputs into this essay.

I thank Paullumi Mukheerjee for helping me bring Wajid Ali's *pari* to life.


### References


Sharar, Abdul Halim, 1975, *Lucknow: The Last Phase of an Oriental Culture*, tr. and ed. E.S. Harcourt and Fakhir Hussain, Oxford: Oxford University Press.

Qureshi, Aslam, 1987, *Wajid Ali Shah's Theatrical Genius*, Lahore: Vanguard Books.

Dadheech, Puru and Vibha Dadheech, 2009, *Nritya Nibandh*, New Delhi: Bindu Prakashan.

Bhatt, Ravi, 2006, *The Life and Time of the Nawabs of Lucknow*, New Delhi: Rupa Publications.

Massey, Reginald, 1999, *Indias Kathak Dance: Past, Present, Future*, New Delhi: Abhinav Publications.

Llewellyn-Jones, Rosie, 2014, *The Last King in India Wajid Ali Shah*, Gurgaon: Random House India.

Taqi, Roshan and Krishna Mohan Saxena (trs), 1987, *Bani by Wajid Ali Shah*, Lucknow: Sangeet Natak Akademi.

Subrahmanyam, Padma, 1979, *Bharata's Art: Then and Now*, Bombay: Bhulabhai Memorial Institute.

Praveen, Yogesh (tr.), 1989, *Naajo by Wajid Ali Shah*, Lucknow: Sangeet Natak Akademi.


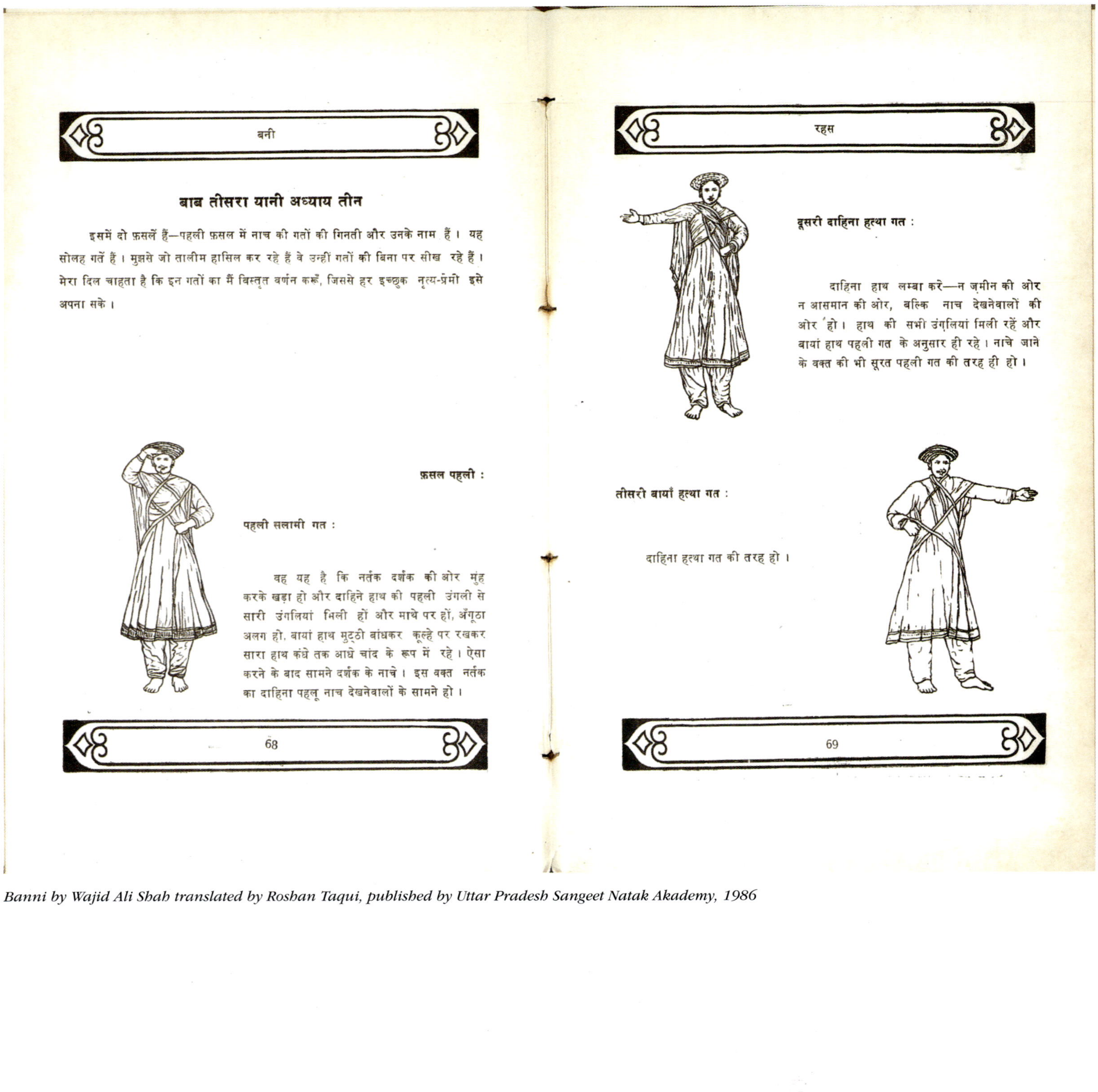

बनी

**बाब तीसरा यानी अध्याय तीन**

इसमें दो फ़सलें हैं—पहली फ़सल में नाच की गतों की गिनती और उनके नाम हैं। यह सोलह गतें हैं। मुझसे जो तालीम हासिल कर रहे हैं वे उन्हीं गतों की बिना पर सीख रहे हैं। मेरा दिल चाहता है कि इन गतों का मैं विस्तृत वर्णन करूँ, जिससे हर इच्छुक नृत्य-प्रेमी इसे अपना सके।

**फ़सल पहली :**

**पहली सलामी गत :**

वह यह है कि नर्तक दर्शक की ओर मुंह करके खड़ा हो और दाहिने हाथ की पहली उंगली से सारी उंगलियां मिली हों और माथे पर हों, अँगूठा अलग हो, बायां हाथ मुट्ठी बांधकर कूल्हे पर रखकर सारा हाथ कंधे तक आधे चांद के रूप में रहे। ऐसा करने के बाद सामने दर्शक के नाचे। इस वक्त नर्तक का दाहिना पहलू नाच देखनेवालों के सामने हो।

68

रहस

**दूसरी दाहिना हत्था गत :**

दाहिना हाथ लम्बा करे—न ज़मीन की ओर न आसमान की ओर, बल्कि नाच देखनेवालों की ओर हो। हाथ की सभी उंगलियां मिली रहें और बायां हाथ पहली गत के अनुसार ही रहे। नाचे जाने के वक्त की भी सूरत पहली गत की तरह ही हो।

**तीसरी बायाँ हत्था गत :**

दाहिना हत्था गत की तरह हो।

69

*Banni by Wajid Ali Shah translated by Roshan Taqui, published by Uttar Pradesh Sangeet Natak Akademy, 1986*

# Portraits of Nawab Wajid Ali Shah

**Malini Roy**

Amongst the extensive holdings at the British Library including visual resources relating to the history of Awadh, there are only a few historic manuscripts, paintings and photographs that document the last king of Awadh, Wajid Ali Shah (1822-87) during his rule and while in exile in Calcutta. The photographic portraits of Wajid Ali Shah and members of his extended family taken by local photographer Ahmad Ali Khan (active 1850s-1862) have become increasingly well known in the last two decades through a range of publications and exhibitions.[1] However, a pair of portraits reported to be the two young sons of Wajid Ali Shah, that had been in private hands until acquired by the British Library in February 2018, have remained almost unheard of until now. This essay aims to provide an overview of the Library's collections that related to the artistic production and commissions that date to Wajid Ali Shah's time, many of which require further investigation and analysis.

The earliest watercolour featuring Wajid Ali Shah is a historic visual document, recording the visit of the Governor-General of India Lord Hardinge to Lucknow in November 1847, just ten months after Wajid Ali Shah succeeded as king following the death of his father. The painting by an unknown artist depicts Wajid Ali Shah in *durbaar*, embracing, Lord Hardinge. As the purpose of Hardinge's visit to Lucknow was to cajole the king and his ministers to act accordingly or else the British would annex the state, it is surprising that the artist in fact portrayed a rather jovial greeting between the two men. The scene takes place in the Chattar Manzil where both British civil and military offices are present. According to Mildred Archer, the picture "may depict the presentation of new standards to the Awadh troops by the British on the occasion of the king's accession".[2]

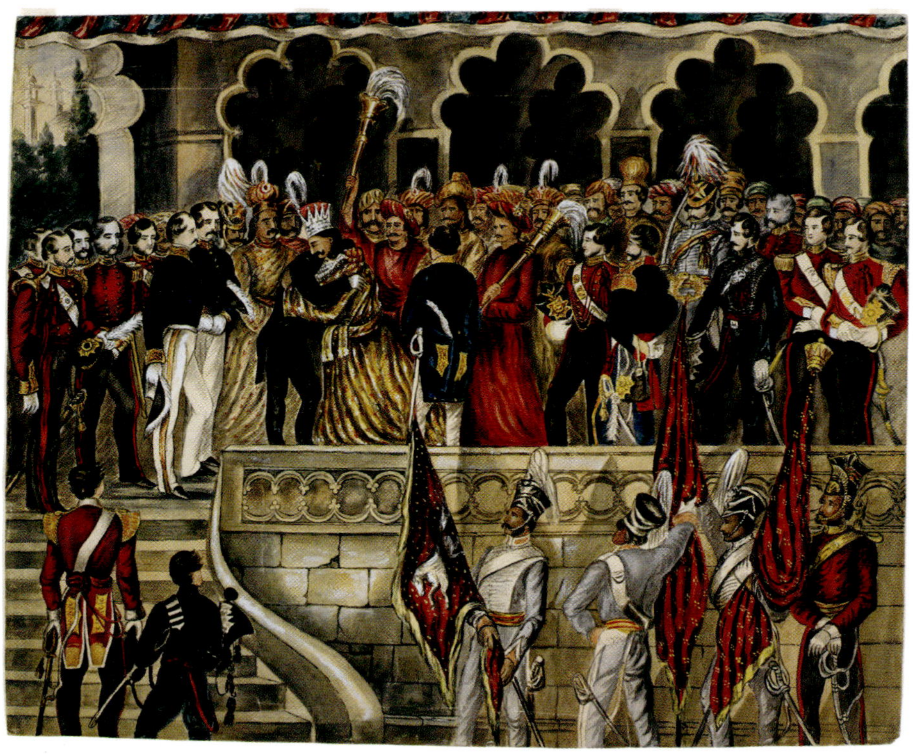

*Image 1: Durbar scene showing Wajid Ali Shah (king of Awadh 1847-56) embracing the Governor-General, Lord Hardinge by an unknown artist in Lucknow, c.1847. Watercolour on paper 19 x 23.5 inches. British Library, Add Or 742*

One of the best known illustrated manuscripts that date to this period is undoubtedly the Windsor Castle's *Ishqnamah* (*Chronicle of Love*), the poetical work composed in Urdu by the *nawab* himself narrating his life at court and his affairs of love with his wives and consorts. This illustrated manuscript, consisting of 103 illustrations, dates to 1849-50, featuring him as a youthful man of no older than 27. The manuscript is distinctive with not only its sumptuous illustrations of the palace's interior, but also the lavish marginal illuminations in gilt, with the royal arms at the top of pages. Stylistically, the *Ishqnamah* acts as a marker to lesser-known manuscripts composed by Wajid Ali Shah that were produced during the 1850s, including two Urdu poetical *masnavis* held in the British Library. The first two manuscripts, the *Bahr-i Ulfat* (*Ocean of Love*) and *Darya-yi Ta'ashshuq* (*The Impassioned Sea*), each features an illuminated frontispiece depicting an enthroned Wajid Ali Shah seated on a European-style golden chair with his feet propped up on a footstool. In both portrait studies, the artists followed a standardized convention of the king adorned with a crown with two standard-bearers standing directly behind the throne holding peacock feather fly whisks. While both manuscripts are undated, based on his countenance and the similarities of wearing his hair in long curls, the portraits suggest a date of pre-1856 and before he left for Calcutta.

In addition to the two manuscripts above, there is a third volume with a portrait of Wajid Ali Shah; the volume consists of a mixture of the king's letters in Persian and Urdu that were sent to his consort Mumtaz Jahan, titled *Ta'rikh-i Mumtaz* (*The Choicest of Histories*). While the manuscript is dated to 1859, the portrait itself recalls the grandeur of the Lucknow court. The rather heavyset ruler is pictured enthroned in a grandiose circular golden throne complete with a short flight of steps to access the platform. Artists featured this style of throne in an illustration documenting the accession of Amjad Ali Shah in the Windsor *Ishqnamah* as well as in a scene showing the formal throne room in the Lal Baradari, Chattar Manzil in Lucknow. Standing behind the ruler are four women, of which two hold peacock feather fly whisks, the imperial emblem of royalty.

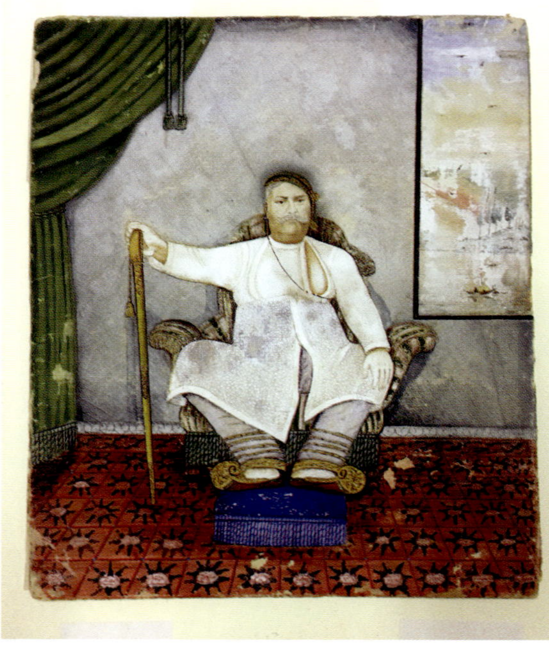

*Image 2: Wajid Ali Shah, King of Awadh by Muhammad Jan (fl. 1860s), c.1865. Painted in Calcutta. Gouache with gold on paper, 19.8 x 17.1 cm. British Library, Add Or 3768*

The next two portraits of Wajid Ali Shah date to his period of exile in Garden Reach, the suburb of Calcutta following the annexation of Awadh by the British. The first portrait is by the artist Muhammad Jan of Lucknow [*Image* 2], though painted in Calcutta in *c.*1865. This distinctive portrait features an older Wajid Ali Shah with a short cap of grey hair as opposed to his lustrous black curls that are ironically featured in the previously mentioned portraits. He is dressed in a simple embroidered white muslin *jama* and *pyjamas* with decadent curved toe slippers. Again, the king is featured seated in a European-style armchair with his feet raised on a footstool. The verso of the painting is inscribed in Persian: "portrait of King Wajid Ali Shah presented by me, daughter of Ali Bandi and the painter Amir Husain of Banairah, [son or pupil of] Muhammad Jan, Court Painter of Matia Burj". On examining related materials in printed publications, it appears that Muhammad Jan was in fact basing his portrait on a photograph produced in this period showing Wajid Ali Shah in the identical stance, with his right hand resting on the hilt of a walking stick and the same curled toe slippers. The Alkazi Collection of Photography in Delhi holds a copy of the photograph. It is most likely that the court artist accompanied the king to Calcutta and prepared the painting during the 1860s.

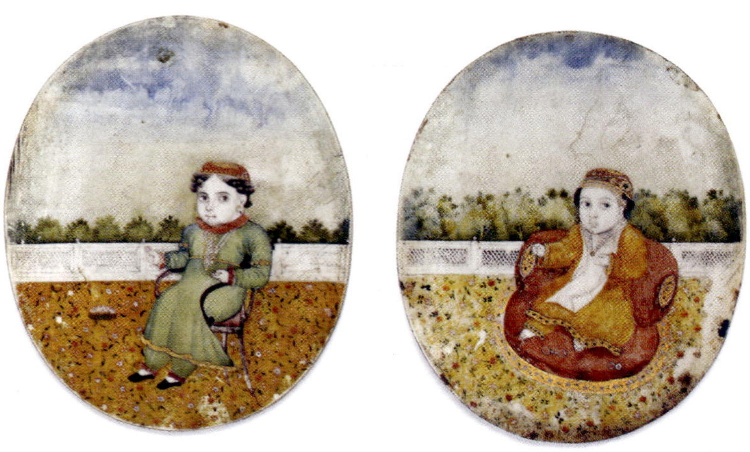

*Image 3: Two portraits on ivory of the sons of Wajid Ali Shah, by an unknown artist in Lucknow, c.1840-42. Watercolour on ivory. 10.5 x 8.2 cm each. Add Or 5770-5771.*

The second of the two portraits of Wajid Ali Shah in exile is by the British amateur artist Major-General Herbert Charles (1820-97). The pen-and-ink sketch on blue paper, picturing just the head and shoulders of the elderly king is more of a caricature than a polished portrait study. The added inscription, "H.M. The King of Oudh from life. 14 Augt 1867. CH" is helpful in tracing the shifts in the physiognomy of the ruler during his later years in exile.

While the illustrated manuscripts and the select loose images document Wajid Ali Shah's physiognomy, there is limited visual documentation on his extended family, however, this would have been the norm in terms of artistic commissions. In fact, one could say, that due to Wajid Ali Shah's narcissistic personality and all-consuming affairs of love with the women of the court, he was an active patron as far as commissioning portraits of himself and his favourite wives. Furthermore, as evidenced through Ahmad Ali Khan's well-known formal photographs taken in 1855 in Lucknow, directly commissioned by the King of Awadh, photographic prints of two of his wives and her daughter have been documented. The photographer was asked to photograph king's second wife, Akhtar Mahal Nauwab Raunaq-ara (whom he married in 1851) as well as Qaisar Begum, one of his favourite wives, as well as his daughter Nawaub Raj Begum Sahibah. Additionally, Ahmad Ali Khan was able to capture an informal group portrait of Wajid Ali Shah seated on a western style sofa with both his Queen Akhtar Mahal and their unnamed daughter. The depiction of the wives and at least one daughter now directs us to the question of visual records of Wajid Ali Shah's sons and potential heirs to the throne. While the photographs by Amhad Ali Khan in the mid-1850s and by photographer Abbas Ali in the 1870s in his volume *An Illustrated Historical Album of the Rajas and Taaluqdars of Oudh*, do not record any photographs of the sons, one queries if this was a gross oversight by the King of Awadh.

In February 2018, the British Library acquired a pair of small portraits of identified through the accompanying inscriptions as the two young sons of Wajid Ali Shah. The unidentified artist used the traditional European technique of painting directly onto a disc of ivory, using watercolour pigments, a technique adopted by Indian artists since the late eighteenth century. Based on stylistic grounds, these date to *c.*1840-42. On the reverse of the frame, in a nineteenth-century handwriting style, it is written:

> These are said to be the children of the last Nawab of Oude, India. I was given the miniatures by one of his descendants, whose grandfather, after the mutiny, had sought refuge in Bhagdad [*sic*].

The first of the two portraits pictures a young child of no more than twelve months in age, based on the fact that he is pictured being supported by a bolster on the ground and cannot sit up properly. The second of the two portraits, is of a slightly older child of no more than two years in age who is pictured seated in a European style chair. J.P. Losty suggests that these two sitters most likely appear to be of the second and third sons of Wajid Ali Shah, as the firstborn was deaf and mute and hence passed over. The second son being Falak Qadar "a fine looking boy" who would die prematurely of smallpox at the age of eleven and the third son being Hamid Ali (1838-74) would become the prince-apparent. Hamid Ali would later visit Britain in 1857, photographed by Leonida Caldesi at an exhibition in Manchester in July 1857.[12]

### References


[1] See S. Gordon, 2010, "'A Sacred Interest': The Role of Photography in the 'City of Mourning'", in *India's Fabled City: The Art of Courtly Lucknow*, eds S. Markel and B. Gude, pp. 145-63, Los Angeles: Los Angeles County Museum of Art.

[2] See M. Archer, *Company Drawings in the India office,*India Office Library, London, 1972, no. 116.

[3] Royal Library, Windsor Castle, RCIN 1005035.

[4] British Library, Or.70.c.3. See S. Baburi, "Sources for the Study of Muhammad Vajid Ali Shah", *Asian and African Studies Blog*, https://britishlibrary.typepad.co.uk/asian-and-African/2015/01/sources-for-the-study-of-muhammad-vajid-ali-shah.html

[5] British Library, Or.70.c.5. Ibid.

[6] See J.P. Losty, 2003, "Painting at Lucknow, 1775-1850", in *Lucknow: Then and Now*, ed. R. Llewelyn-Jones, Bombay: Marg Publications, fig. 15.

[7] See R. Llewelyn-Jones, 2014, *The Last King in India: Wajid Ali Shah*, London: Hurst & Company, illustration no. 18.

[8] See M. Archer, Company Drawings in the India Office, India Office Library, London, 1972, no. 130. According to Archer, there is a collection of his drawings at Bharat Kala Bhavan, Benares and select works by his son Mammu Jan (d. 1934) in the State Museum in Lucknow.

[9] The inscription of the photograph refers to her by her full title of Mumtaz 'Alam Nauwab Qaisar Mahall Sahibah, see British Library, Photo 500(4).

[10] See S. Gordon, 2010, fig. 16.

[11] R. Llewelyn-Jones, 2014, p. 77

[12] Ibid, illustration no. 3.

# Poetry and Paintings

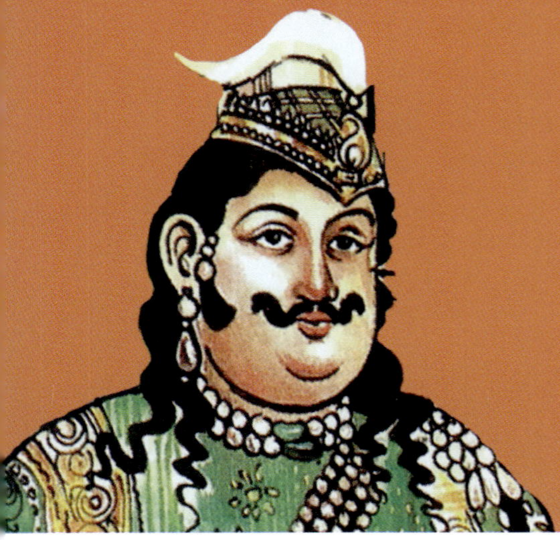

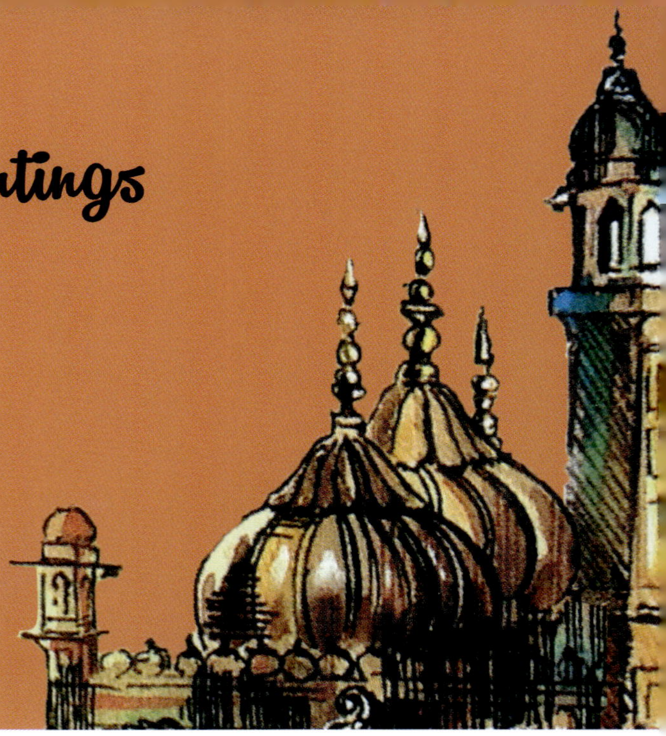

*Translation by*
**Muzaffar Ali**

1

बाबुल मोरा नैहर छूटो जाए।
चार कहार मिल डुलिया मंगावो
मोरा अपना बेगाना छूटो जाए।
अंगना तो पर्वत भया और देहरी भई बिदेस।
ले बाबुल घर आपुनो मैं चली पिया के देस।
मेरा अपना बिगाना छूटो जाए। बाबुल मोरा नैहर छूटो जाए।

पितृगृह से बिछड़ने पर नवविवाहिता का पिता से कथन
हे पिता! आज मेरा पीहर छूटा जा रहा है।
चार कहार मुझे डोली में बिठाकर ले जा रहे हैं।
मेरे सभी परिजन मुझसे बिछुड़ रहे हैं।
अब मेरे लिए घर का आँगन पर्वत के समान कठिन हो गया है,
और दहलीज विदेश हो गई है।
हे पिता! अब यह घर तुम्हारे ही पास रहेगा।
मैं तो अपने प्रियतम के घर जा रही हूँ।

Oh my beloved father!
I am being taken away from your home …
As four men lift my palanquin
I am being wrenched away from my land
From those known and those unknown to me …
The courtyard I played in
Becomes a unscaleable mountain and my threshold an alien land.
Oh my beloved father! now you can keep your home …
as I leave for my Lover's home …

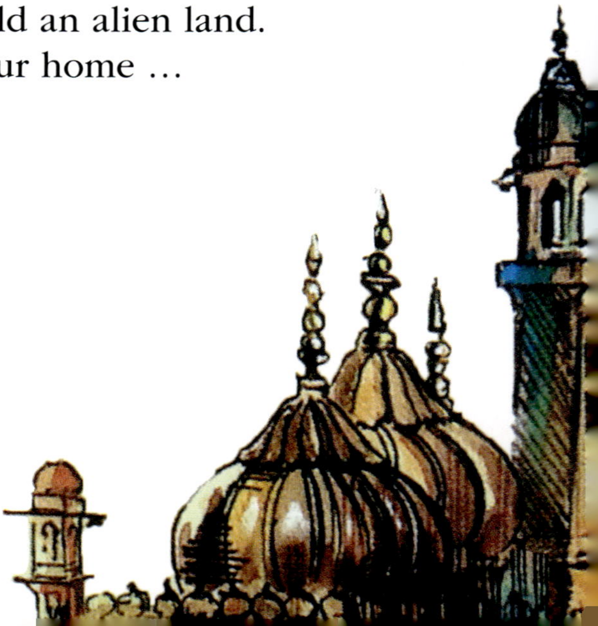

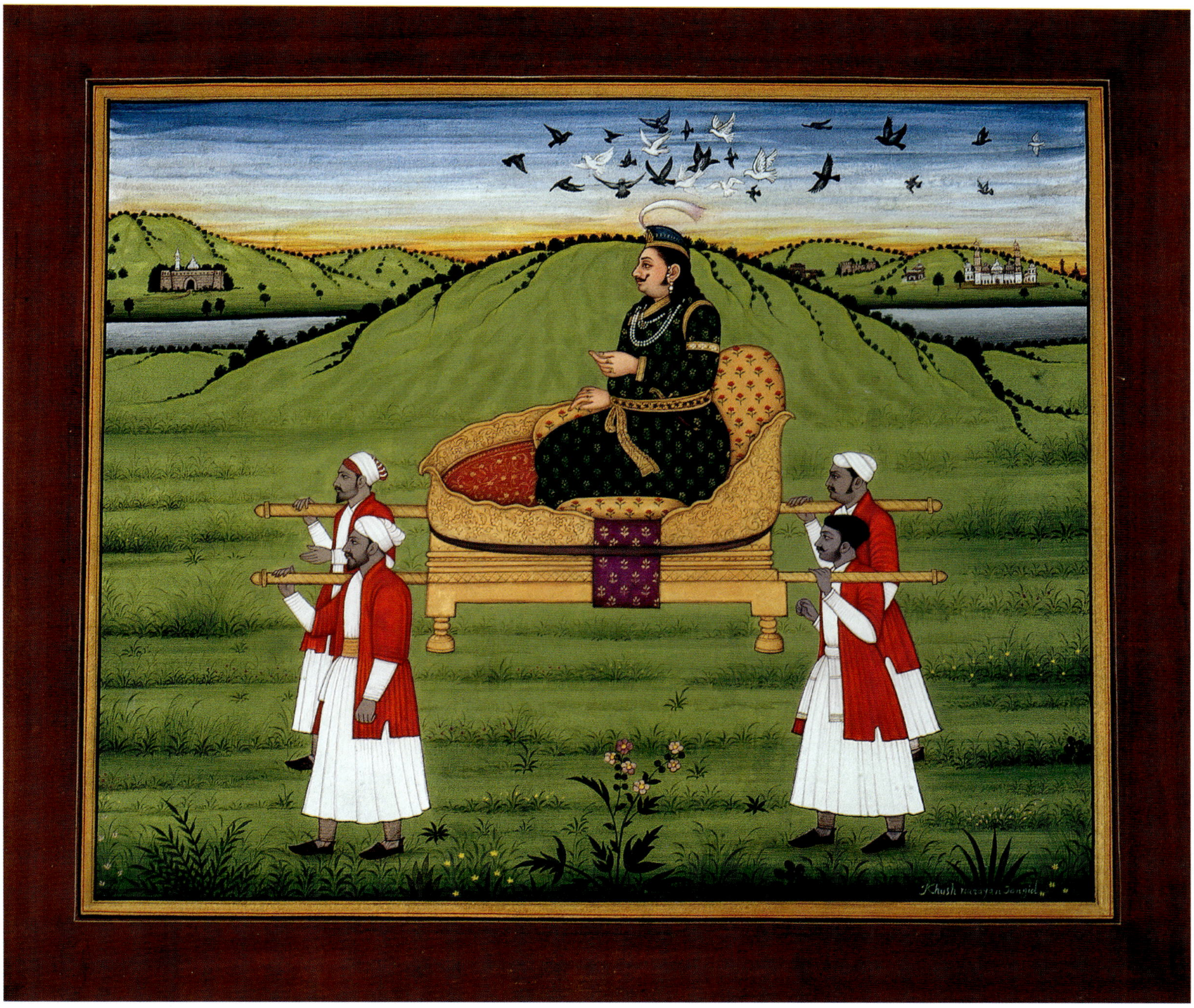

**Artist:** *Khush Narayan Jangid*

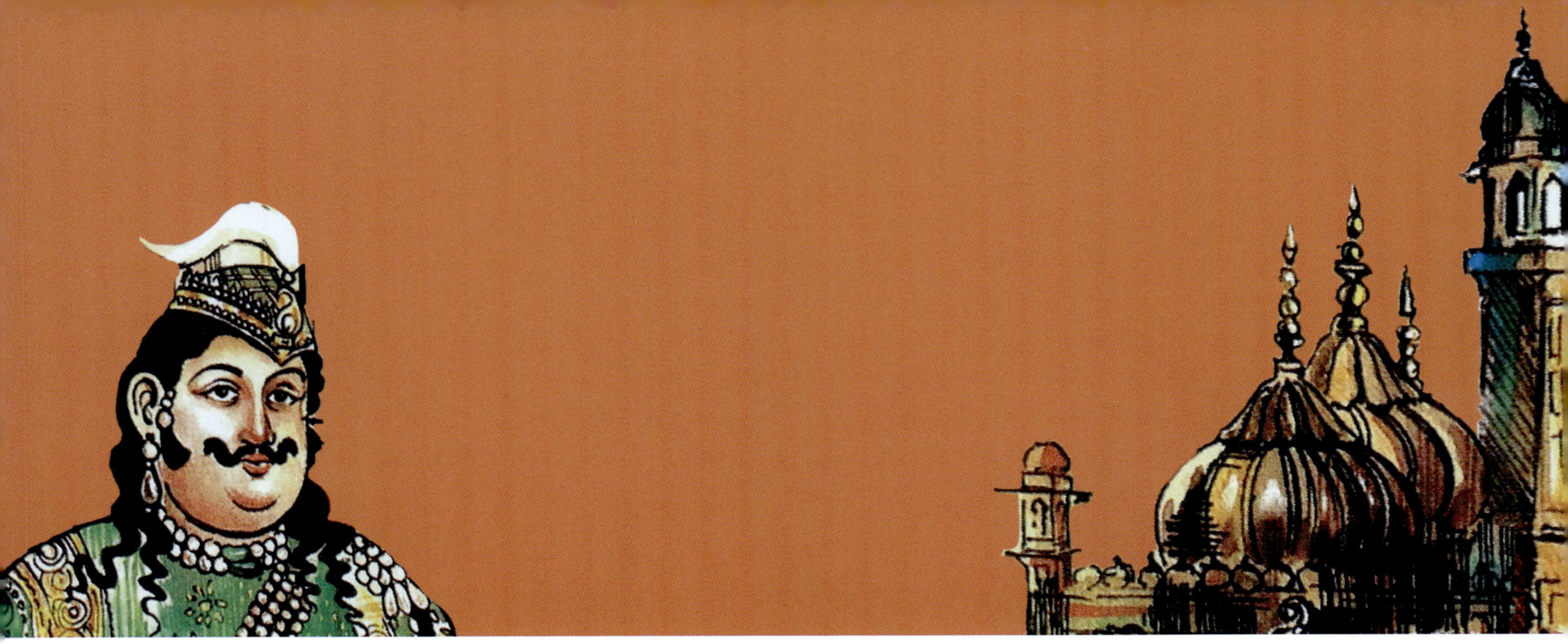

2

मेलबे को जिया मोरा चाहे।
ए री सखी इतनी बिनती मोरी
सुन कहियो जाए।
घड़ी घड़ी पल पल छिन छिन निस दिन
विकल होत जिया तुमरे दरस बिन।
अख़्तर पिया को कोई ले जाए।

प्रियतम से मिलने को मेरा दिल कर रहा है।
हे सखी तुमसे इतनी विनती है कि मेरा संदेश उनसे कह देना।
प्रियतम के दर्शन किए हुए दिन, रात, घड़ी, पल, क्षण बीत गए हैं
और अब व्याकुलता बढ़ रही है।
अब अख़्तर पिया को कोई प्रीतम के पास ले जाए।

I burn in the desire to be with Thee …
Oh my dear friends! take my plea
Tell my beloved
Each passing moment of every passing day
that comes and goes
My heart yearns restlessly
Without seeing their face …
Will someone now
take this Akhtar to thee

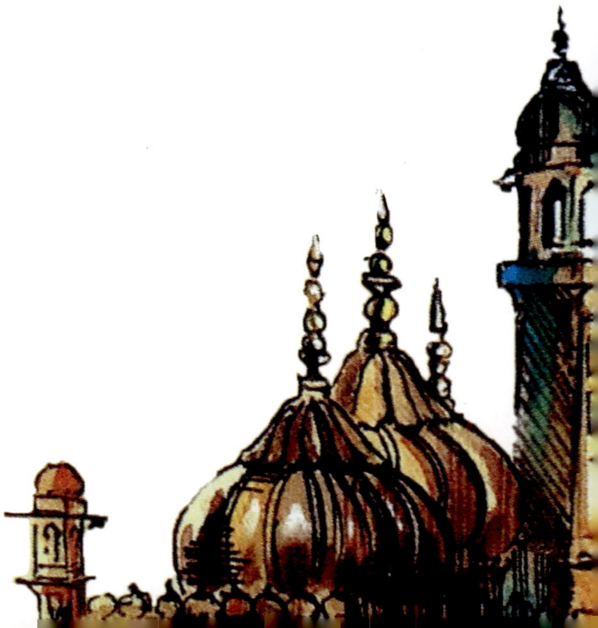

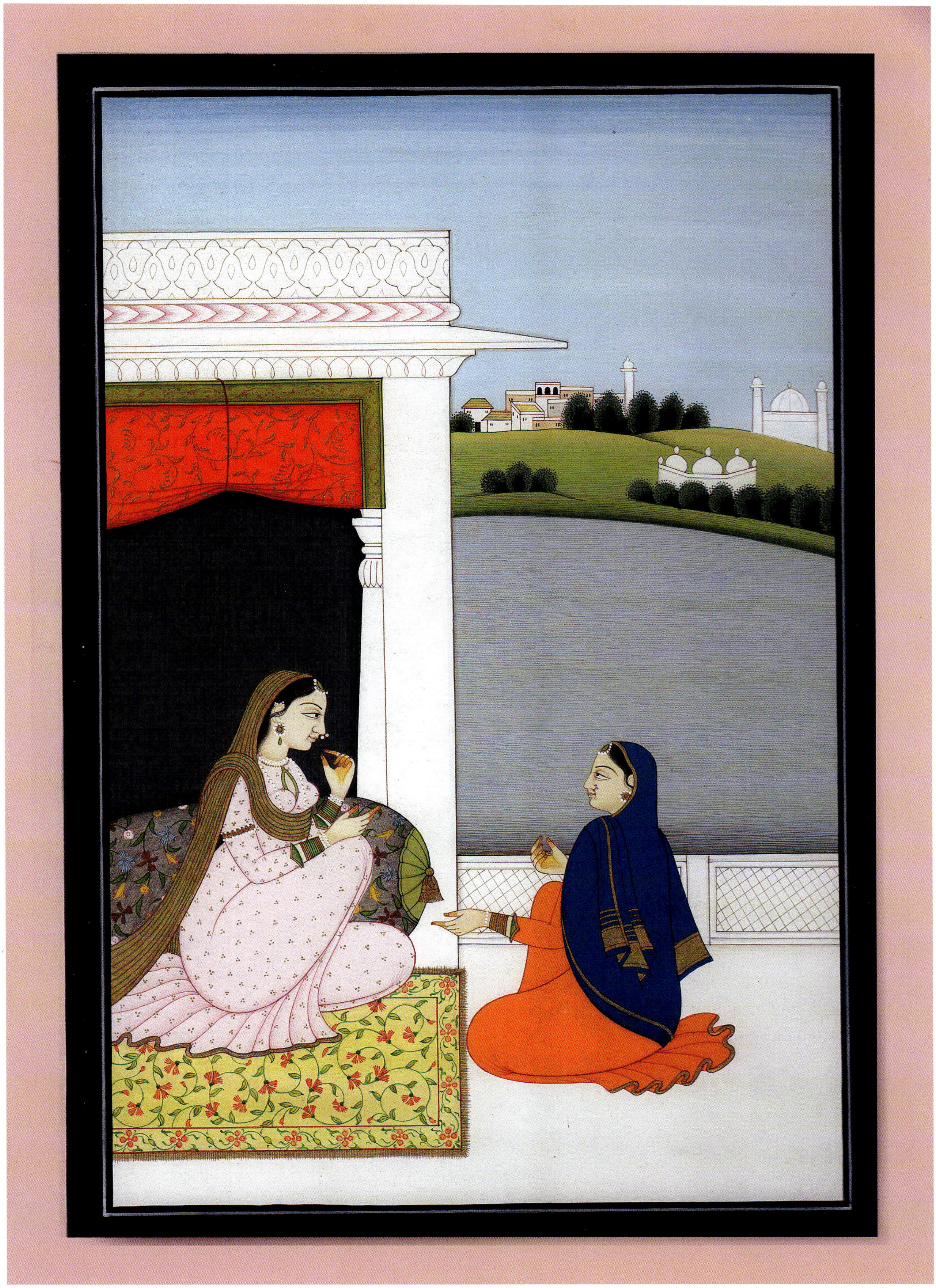

**Artist:** *Deepak Bhandari*

3

फूलवाले कंत मैका बसंत
गरबा मोल दे रे।
अख़्तर पिया सों यूं जा कहिवो
तनक से बिरवा तोड़ दे रे।

हे फूल वाले प्रियतम! वसंत ऋतु में मुझे फूल भेंट कीजिए।
अख़्तर प्रियतम के पास जाकर उन्हें मेरा संदेश कहना कि
पौधों से फूल तोड़कर मुझे दीजिए।

Oh my gardner friend!
Bring flowers to me in bloom
Go for now
tell beloved Akhtar
They must be freshly cut.

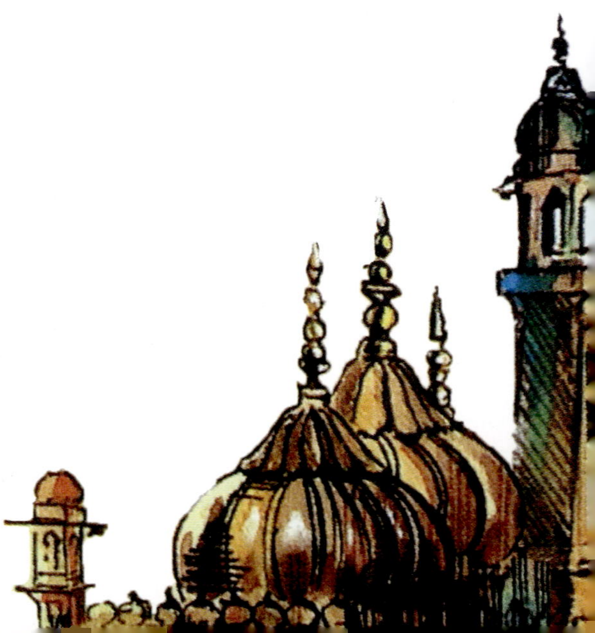

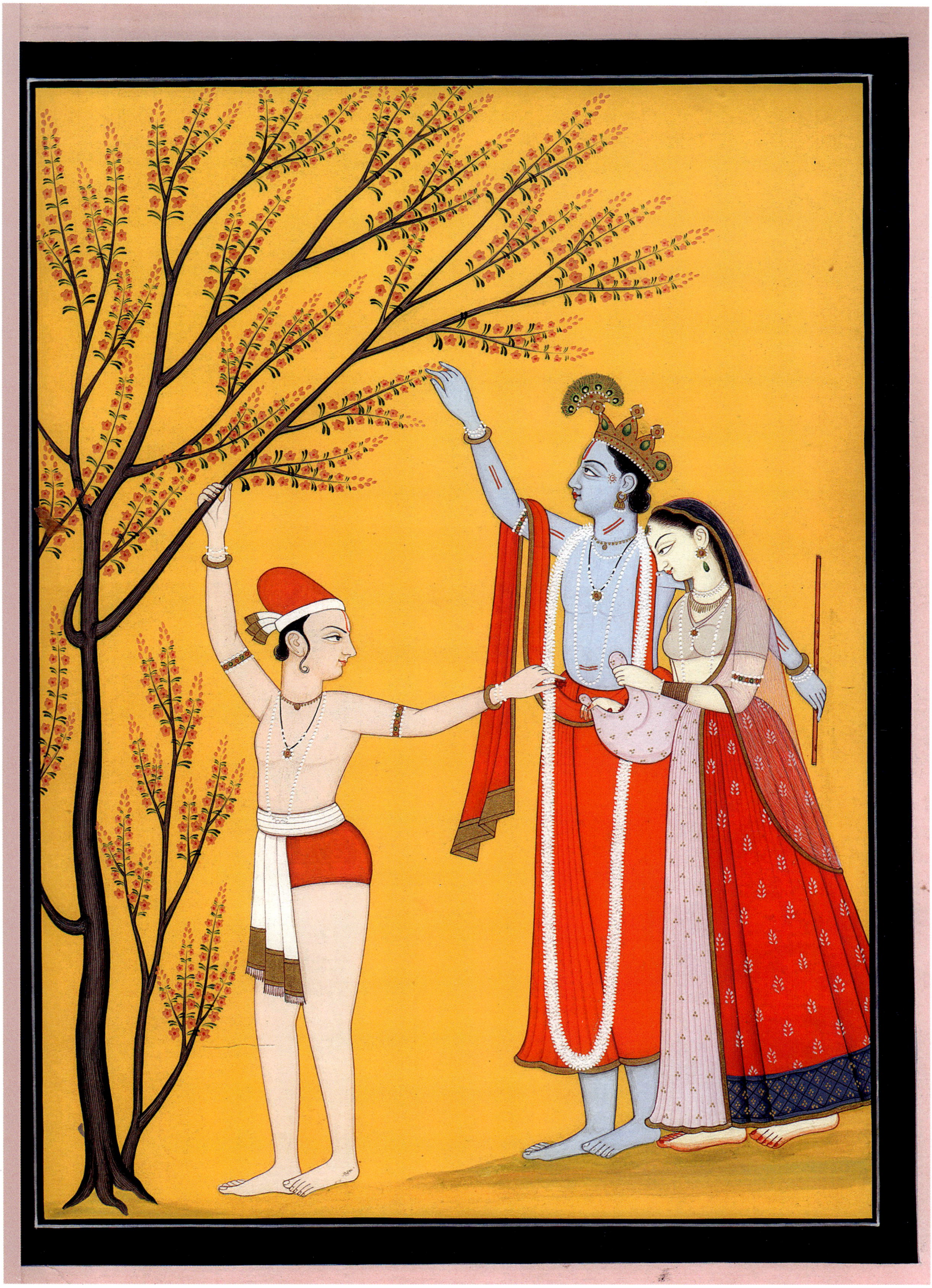

**Artist:** *Vijay Sharma*

4

अंछन मारे लिए प्राण लिए
सुध भूल गई भई बाबरिया रे।
बयारी कमाना जोबन लचके
गोल गोल मृग नयन रसीले।
दरसन जिया चाहत हमारो
अख़्तर का मिलना कठिन भयो रे।

हे प्रियतम, तुमने मुझ पर ऐसी दृष्टि डाली कि अब मैं सुध-बुध खोकर बावरी हो गई हूँ। मेरा बैरी यौवन अपने चरम पर है, और मृग के समान गोल नेत्रों में रस भर गया है। मेरे मन में तुम्हारे दर्शन की प्रबल इच्छा है, लेकिन अब अख़्तर से मिलना मुश्किल हो रहा है।

Your single look leaves me breathless
I lose myself Oh Krishna!
You make me senseless
Your doe like round and sensuous eye ...
My heart yearns for a glimpse of you ...
Akhtar, why is this union so difficult, pray ...

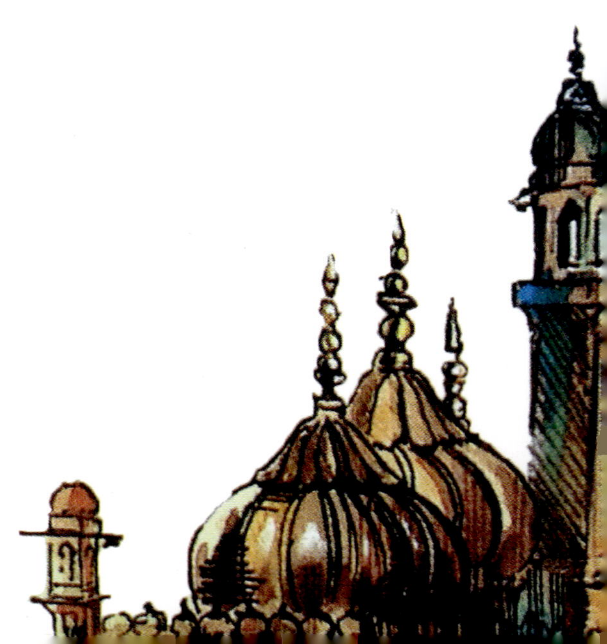

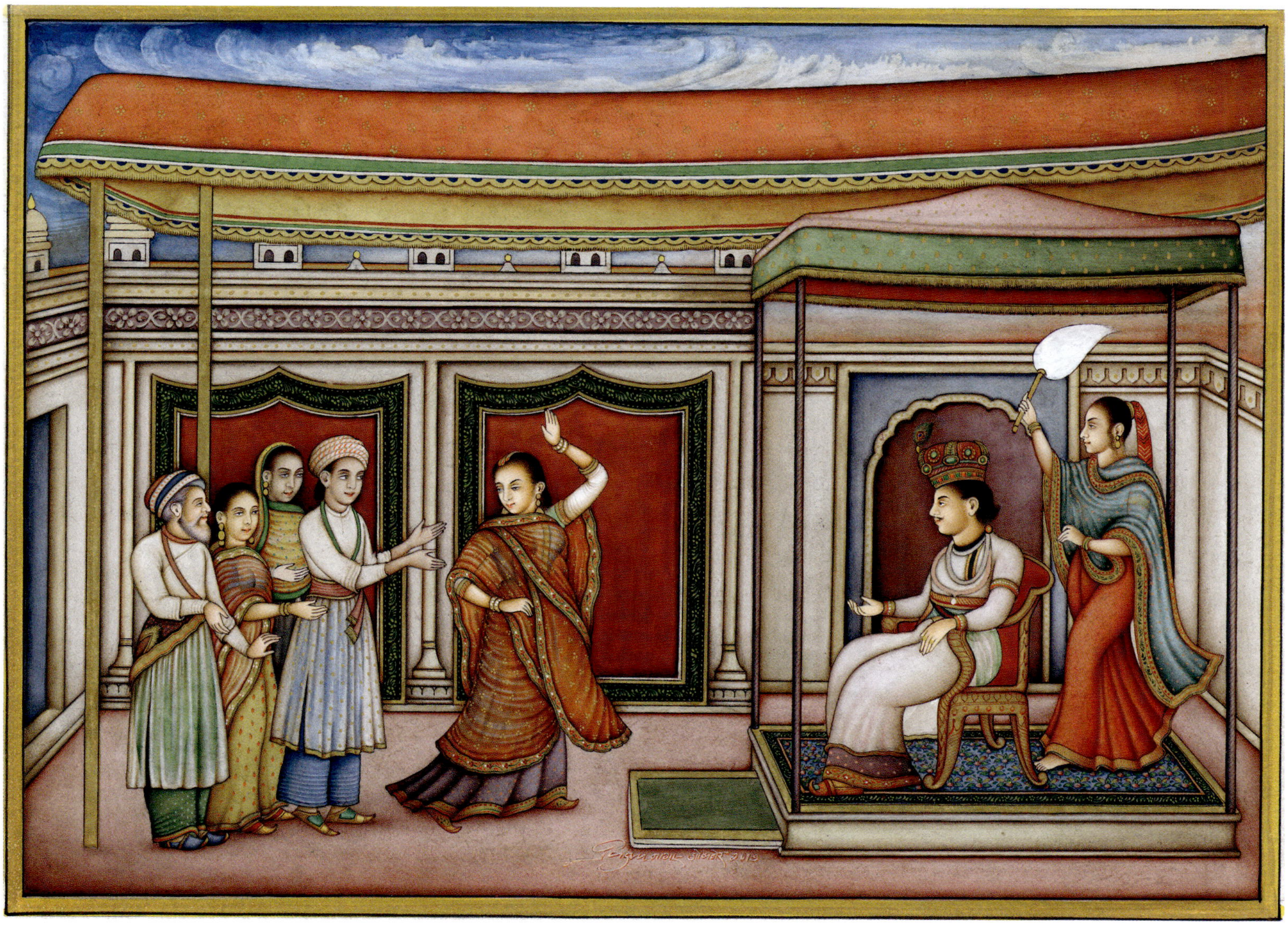

**Artist:** *Vijay Naga*

5

तरप तरप सगरी रैन गुजरी
कौन देस गयो सांवरिया।
भर आई अखियां मतवारी
तरक तरक गई चुनरिया
तुमरे घोड़न मोरे द्वार से जो निकसे
सुध भूल गई मैं बावरिया रे।

सारी रात तड़प-तड़पकर गुजरी है।
ना जाने साँवरिया कौन देश चले गए।
मेरी मतवाली आँखें भर आई हैं और चुनरिया भी फट गई है।
जब से मेरे द्वार के सामने से आपके घोड़े निकले हैं,
मैं तो सारी सुध-बुध भूलकर बावरी हो गई हूँ।

Restless I was
for you all night
to which distant land you've gone
Out of my sight
My saddened eyes well up for thee
The covering on my head is ripped.
Your horses hooves
Resound at my door
I lose myself.

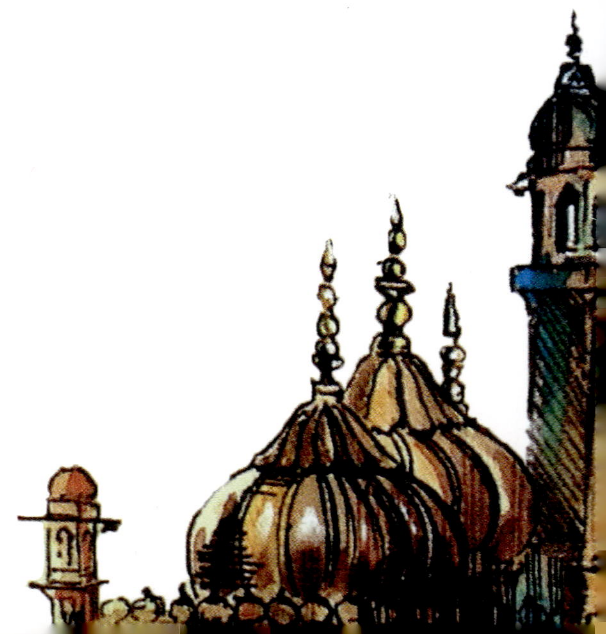

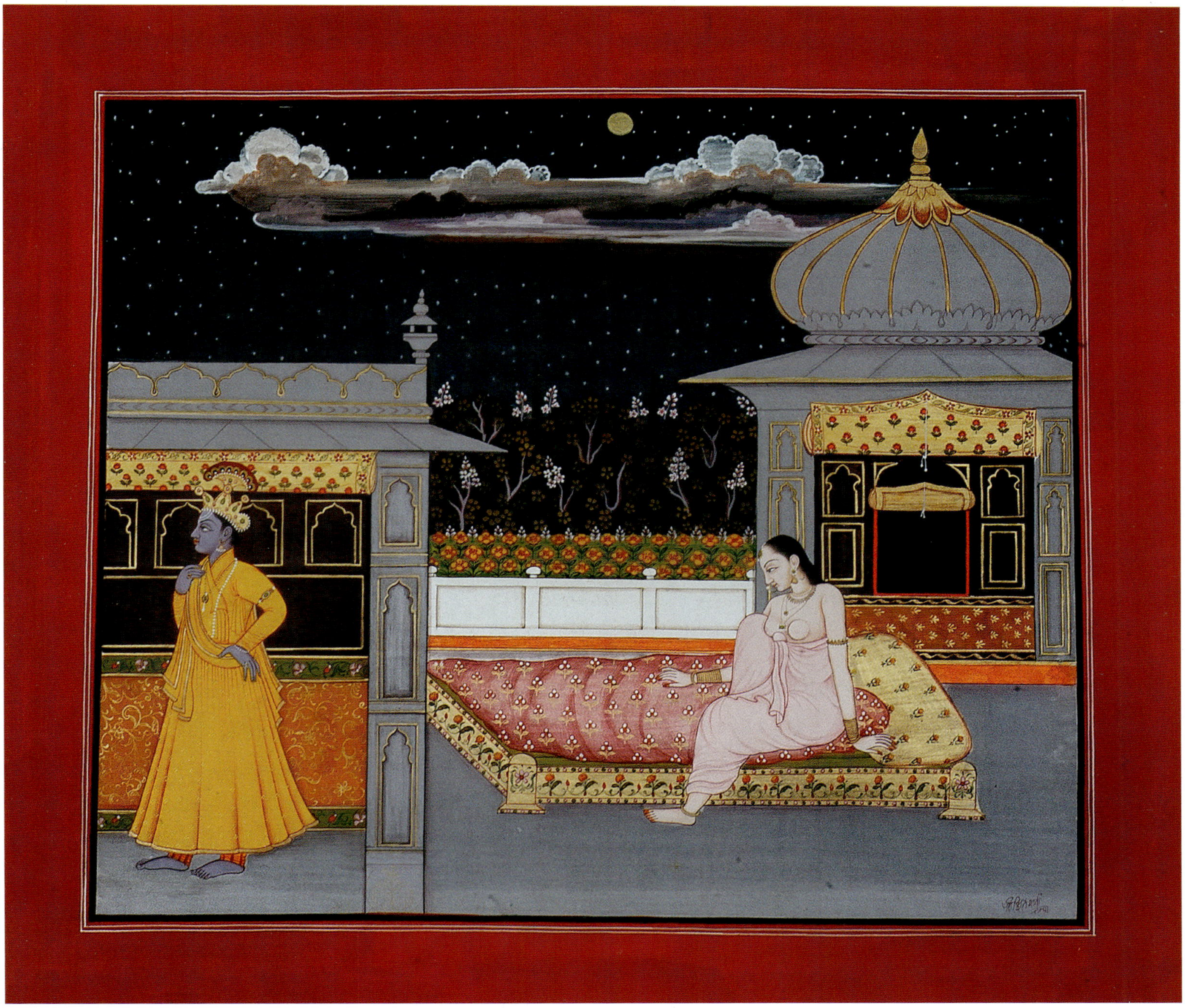

**Artist**: *Parikshit Sharma*

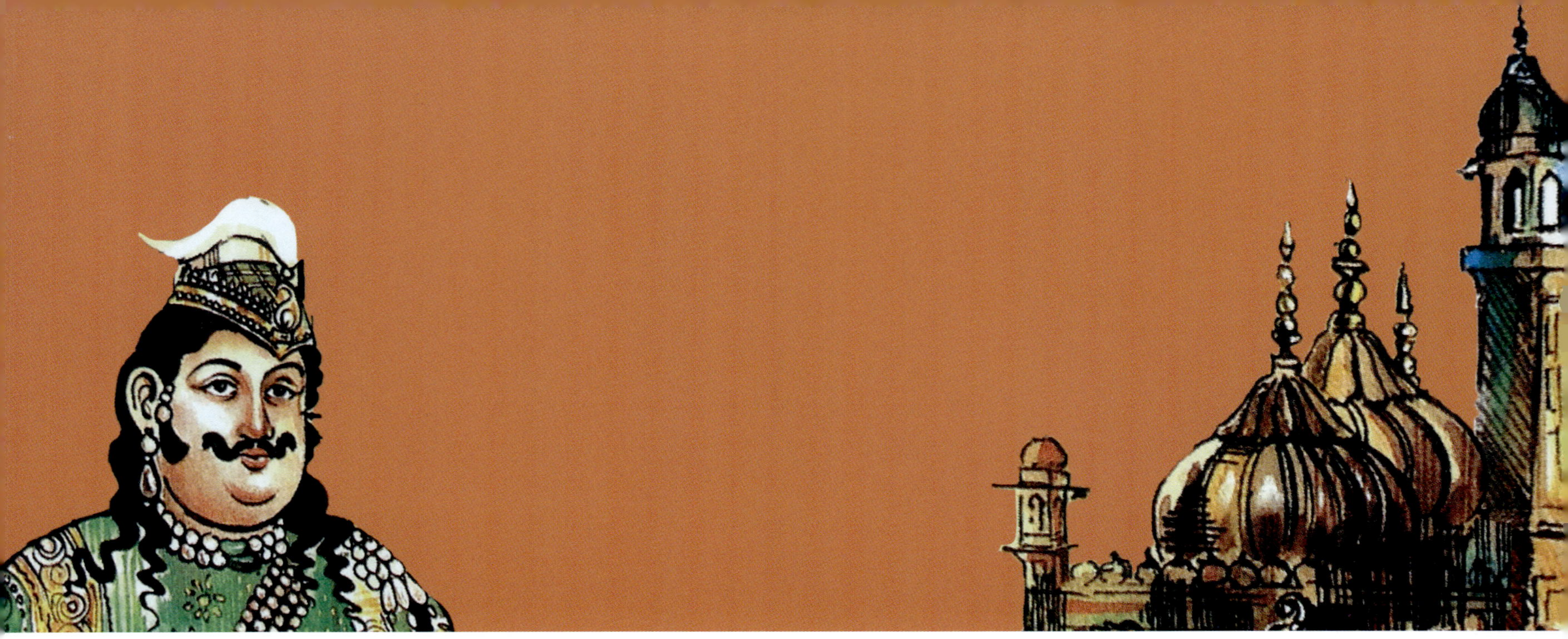

6

नीर भरन कैसे जाऊँ सखी री अब
मोरी डगर चलत मोसे करत रार।
ऐसो चंचल चपल चल हट नटखट
मानत नाही काहू की बात
बिनती करत मैं तो गई रे हार।

हे सखी अब मैं जल भरने कैसे जाऊँ?
राह चलते कृष्ण मुझसे रार करते हैं।
वह ऐसा चंचल, चपल और नटखट है
कि किसी की भी बात नहीं सुनता।
मैं तो विनती करके हार गई हूँ।

My friend! How shall I go to fetch water
On the way Krishna is bound to come and tease me
He is so clever and naughty and he will not listen to anyone
How often have I requested him to spare me
now I have just given up.

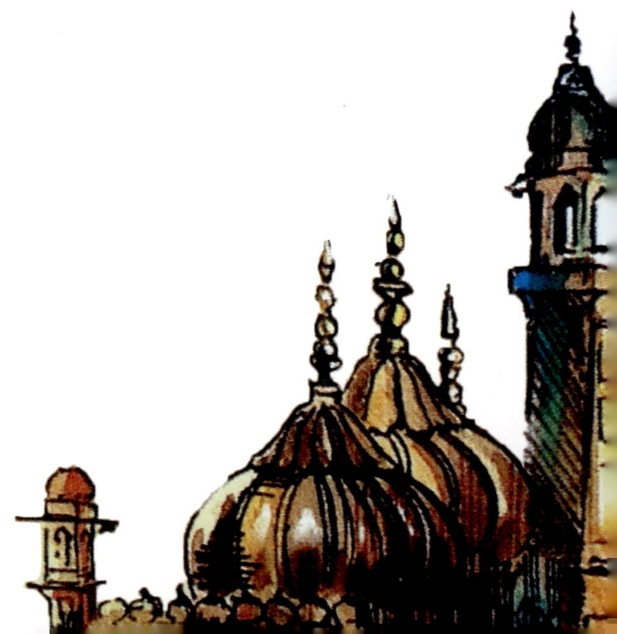

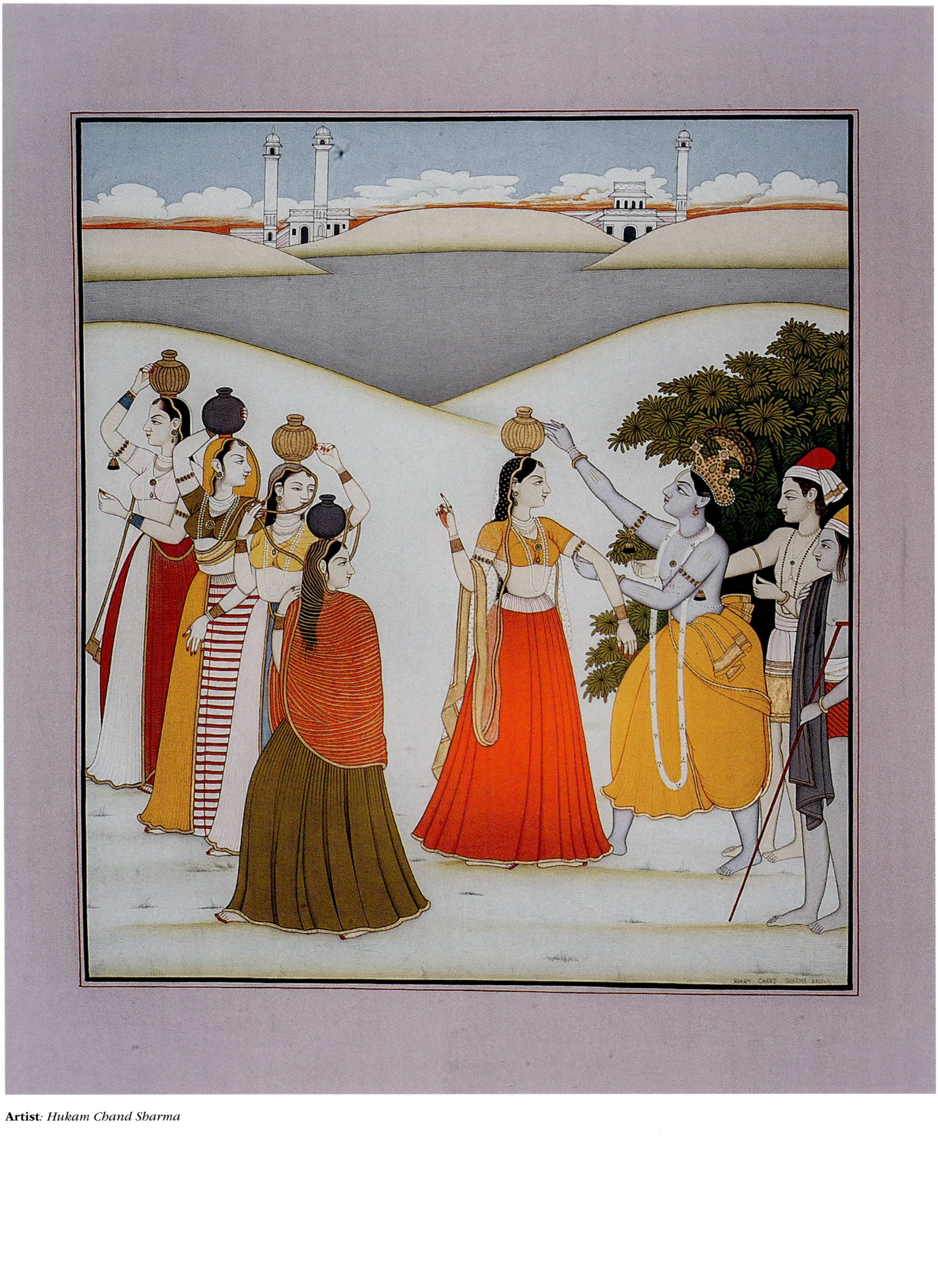

**Artist**: *Hukam Chand Sharma*

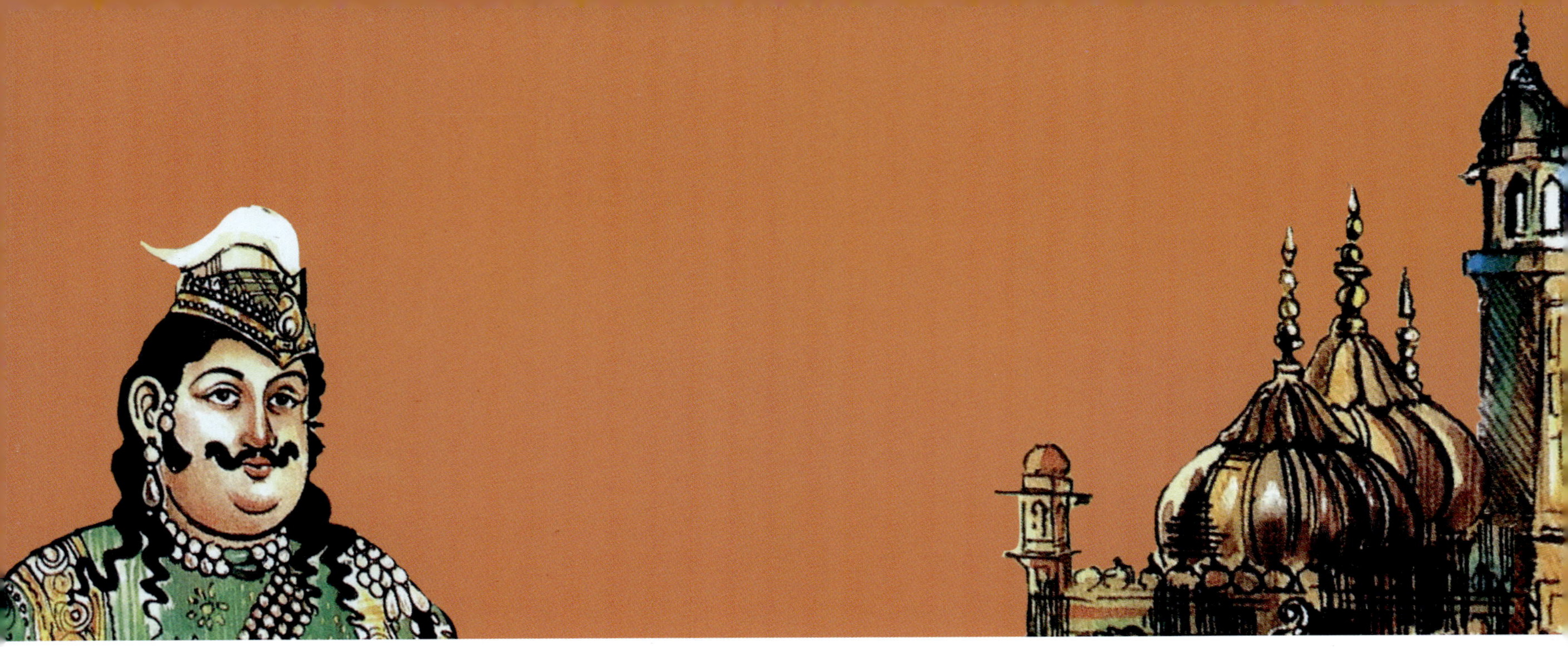

7

मोरी आली मैं पनियाँ कैसे जाऊँ री
सखी री नागर नटखट मुकुटवारौ।
मोसों करत ढिठाई, बंसीबट जमुनातट,
पनियाँ कैसे लाऊँ री॥
उझक उझक और उचक उचक झाँके री अख़्तर,
तट पनघट बंसीबट जमुनातट, पनियाँ कैसे लाऊँ री॥

मेरी सखी! मैं पानी भरने कैसे जाऊँ?
मुकुट वाले नटखट नागर यमुना नदी के तट और बंसीबट पर
मुझसे छेड़खानी करते हैं।
अब मैं पानी कैसे लाऊँ?
अख़्तर! वह पनघट पर उचक-उचककर झाँकता है।
अब मैं पानी कैसे लाऊँ?

Oh my beloved! Oh my friends!
what shall I do
How shall I get the water now
He stands with a crown hell bent on teasing me ...
The arrogant flute player stands firm on the Jamuna banks
How do I fill water now ...
Akhtar jumps up and down to see if he has gone ...
He is still there with his lips on his flute
How do I fill the water now ...

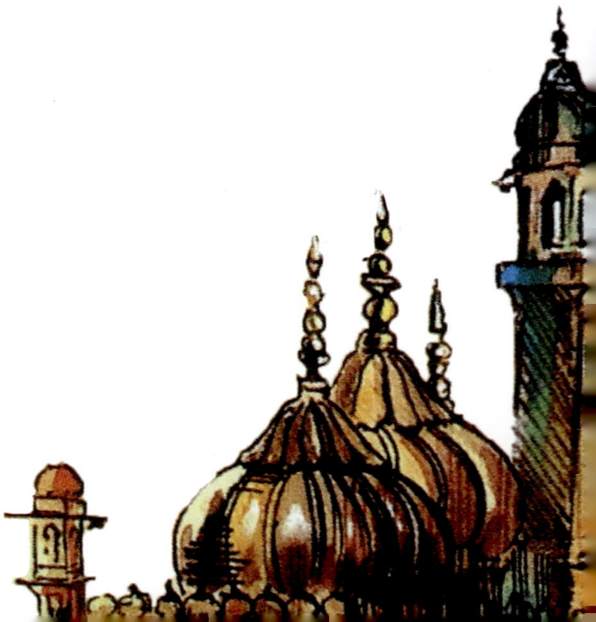

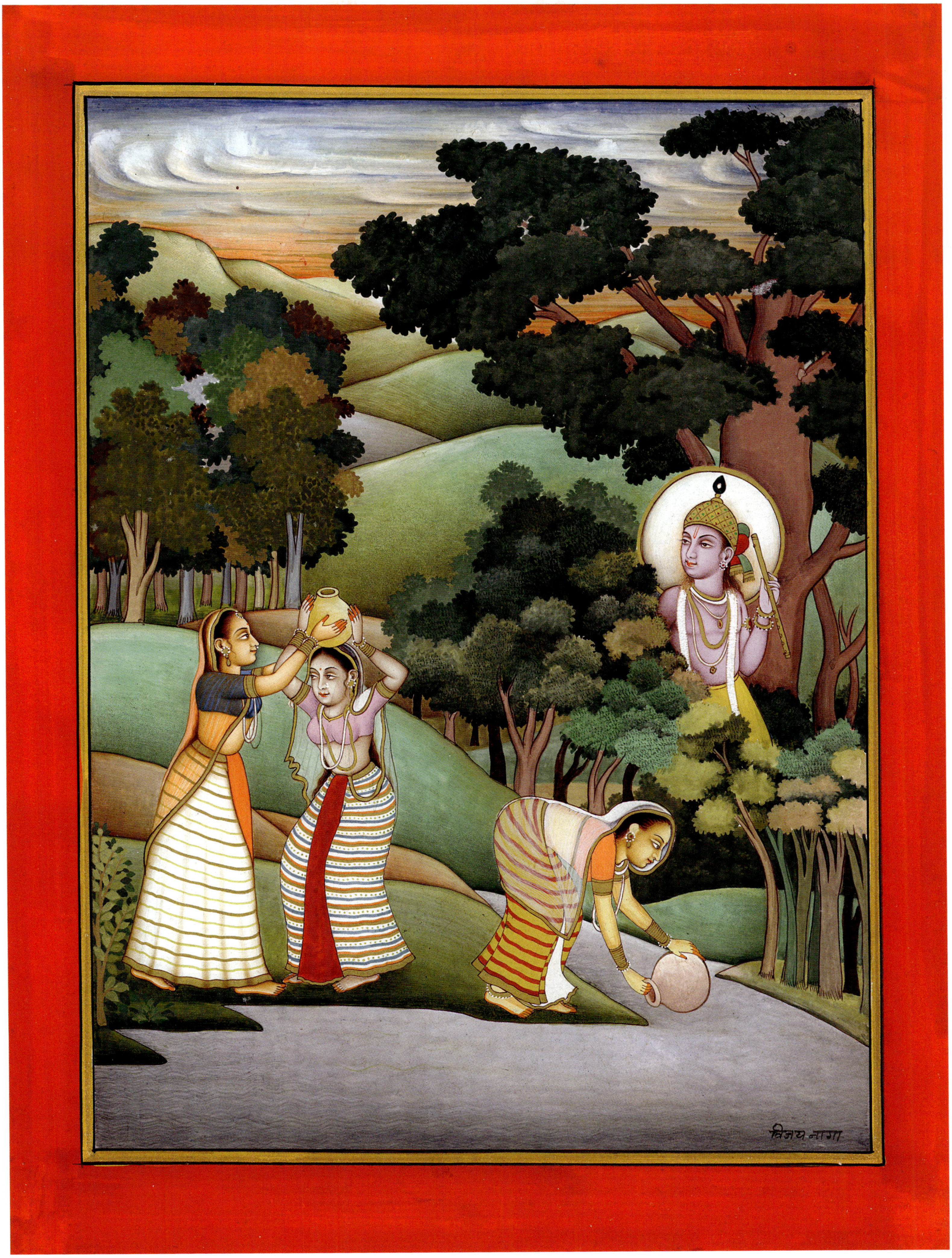


**Artist**: *Vijay Naga*

8

उरझि रहे नैना जोबन पर तुम्हारे ॥
तिरछी नजरिया घायल करि डारो ।
नाम रखो बाँके अख़्तर प्यारे ॥

तुम्हारे यौवन पर मेरे नैना उलझ गए हैं।
तुम्हारी तिरछी नज़र ने मुझे घायल कर दिया है।
प्रियतम का नाम अब बांके अख़्तर रख दो।

Eyes open wide to behold your youth
Your youth that dazzles the eyes ...
Your side glances attack like swords
have wounded me ...
Why don't you give the name Akhtar to your wounded beloved.

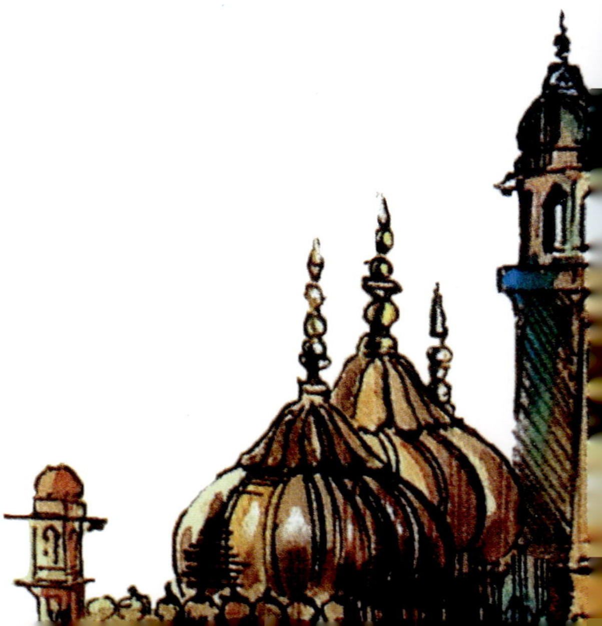

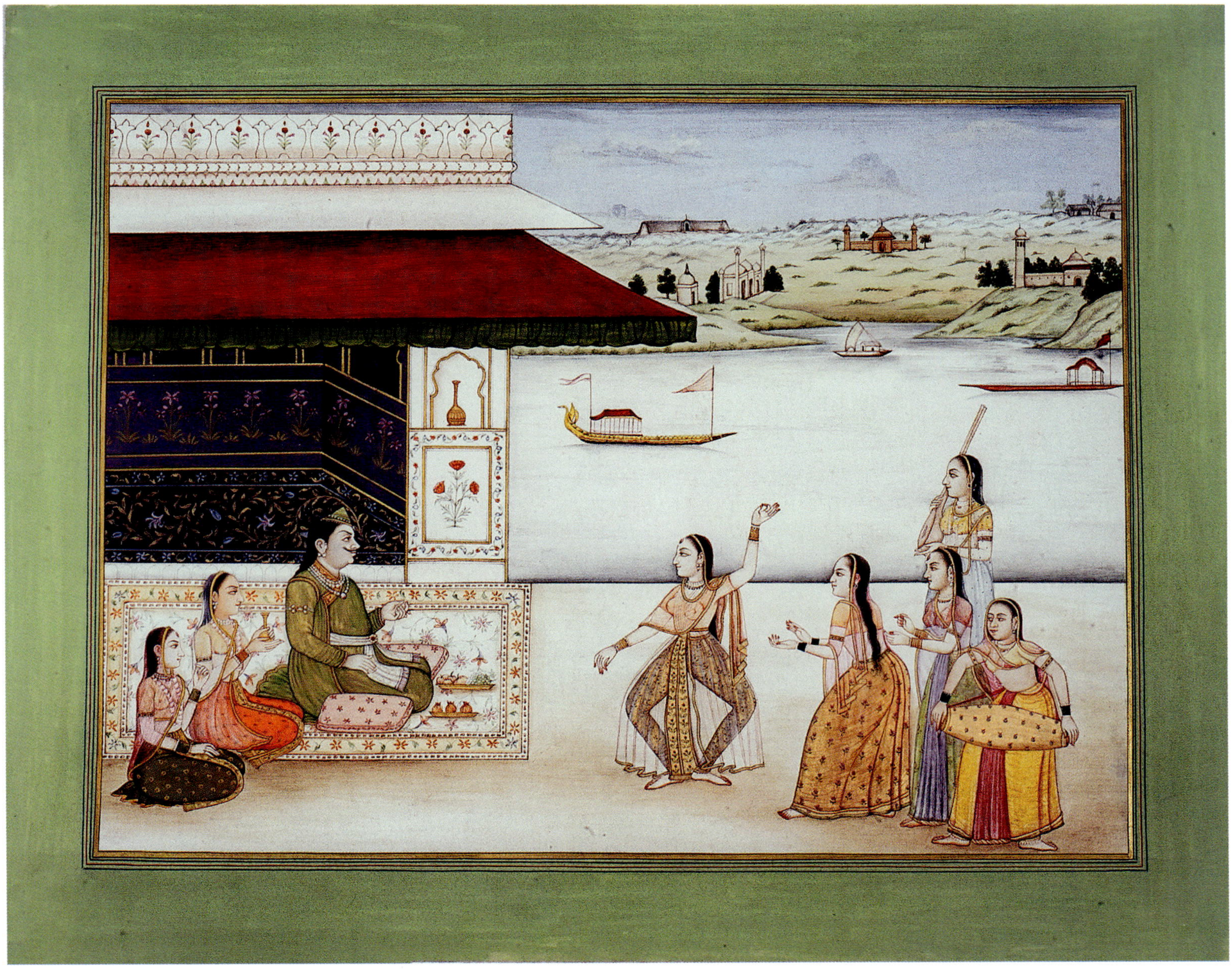

**Artist**: *Mahender Sisodiya*

9

एरी गुइयाँ कैसे भेजूँ पाती क़दर ओर।
काहू को साथी, पाती आप ही चली जाती क़दर ओर।
एक रैन अंधेरी पापिन, सूनी सेज जैसे साँपिन,
कैसे मेरा बारा जियरा, हाय, डसे जाती क़दर ओर॥

मैं "क़दर पिया" को पत्र कैसे भेजूँ?
अच्छा होता कि मेरा प्रेमपत्र खुद चलकर "क़दर" तक पहुँच जाता।
एक तो अँधेरी रात पापिन है, दूसरी ओर सूनी सेज साँपिन के समान है, जो मेरे
नाज़ुक दिल को बेदर्दी से डसी जाती है।

Oh my dear friends!
Tell me how
do I send
a message to my love Kadar Piya
Would it be not
so much better if
somehow
the message will reach
on its own ...
Say the sinful night is dark and eerie
The bed is a bed of snakes ...
All this and more without you
my love
Is a torture
For this helpless heart ...

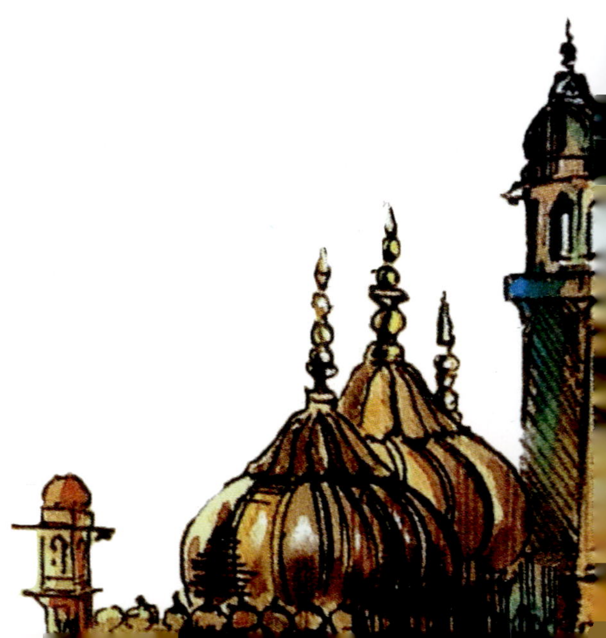

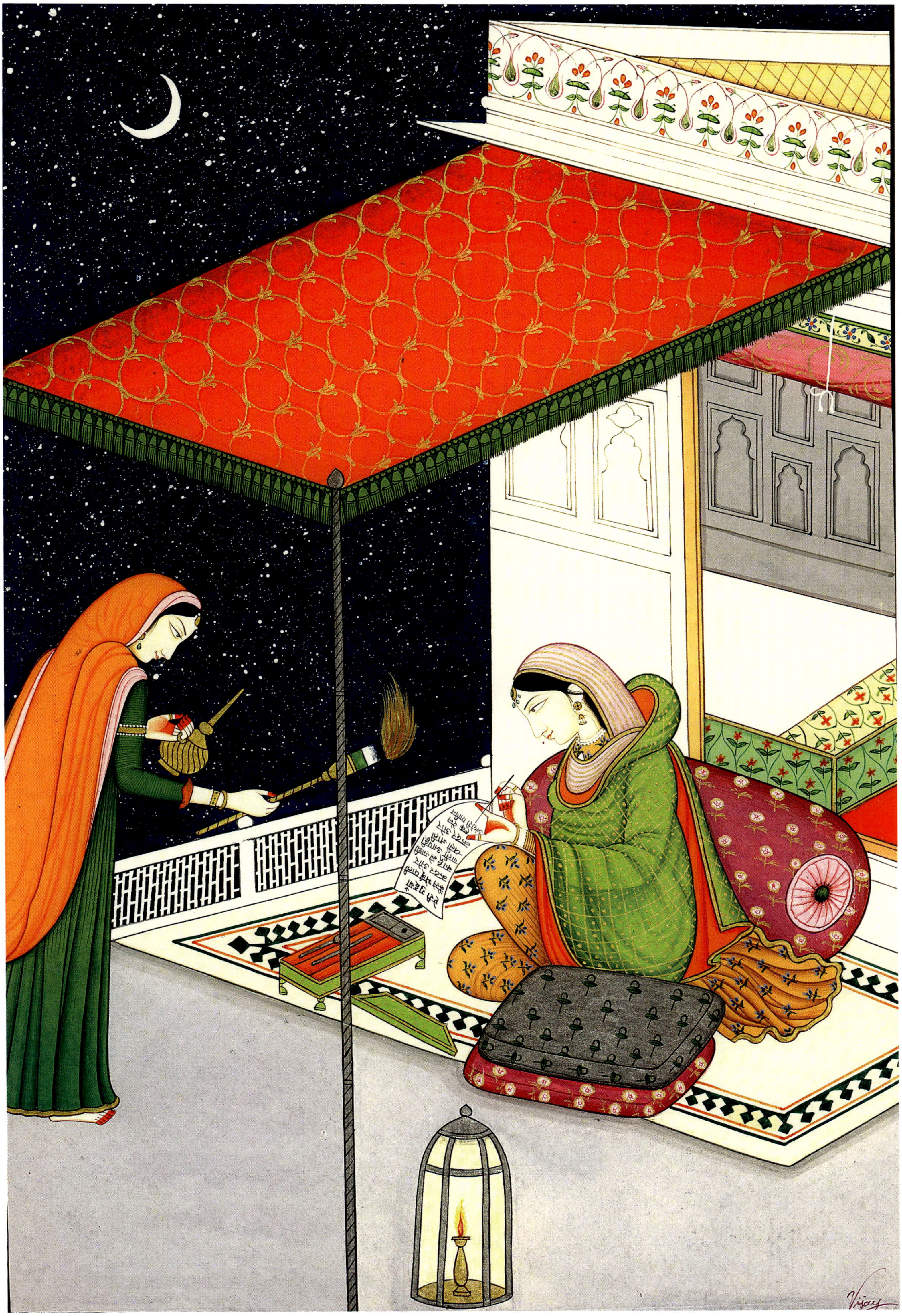

**Artist**: *Vijay Sharma*

10

ठाढ़े रहियो ओ मोरे श्याम ॥
सास ननद को देके दिलासा
चली चलूँगी तो धाम ॥

बिन्दा कहत धीरज मन राखो
करि आऊँ सोलहूं सिंगार ॥

हे श्याम! तुम यहीं खड़े रहना कहीं जाना, मत।
मैं अपनी सास और ननद को दिलासा देकर तुम्हारे घर चलूँगी।
बिंदादीन के अनुसार, राधा चँचल कृष्ण को कहती है कि मन में
धीरज रखो, मैं सोलह सिंगार करके आती हूँ।

Stay there, wait for me
Oh Beloved Shyam!
I have given alibis to my sister and mother-in-law
I am about to head to you ...
Binda says be strong ...
have faith ...
Let me adorn myself for thee ...
Stay there, wait for me
Oh Beloved Shyam!

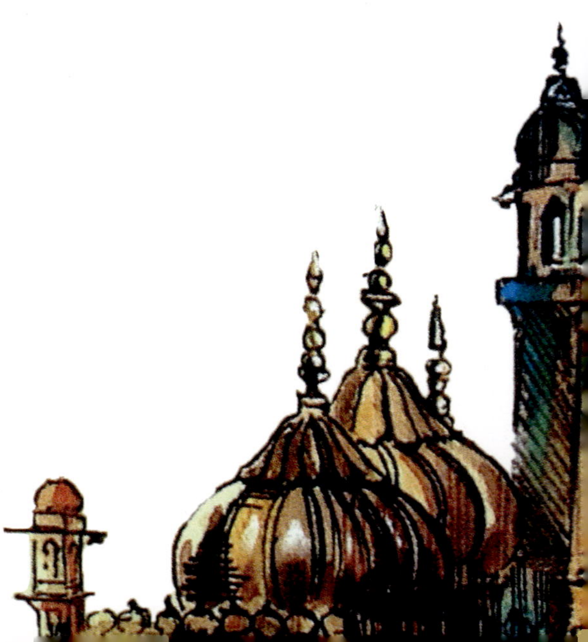

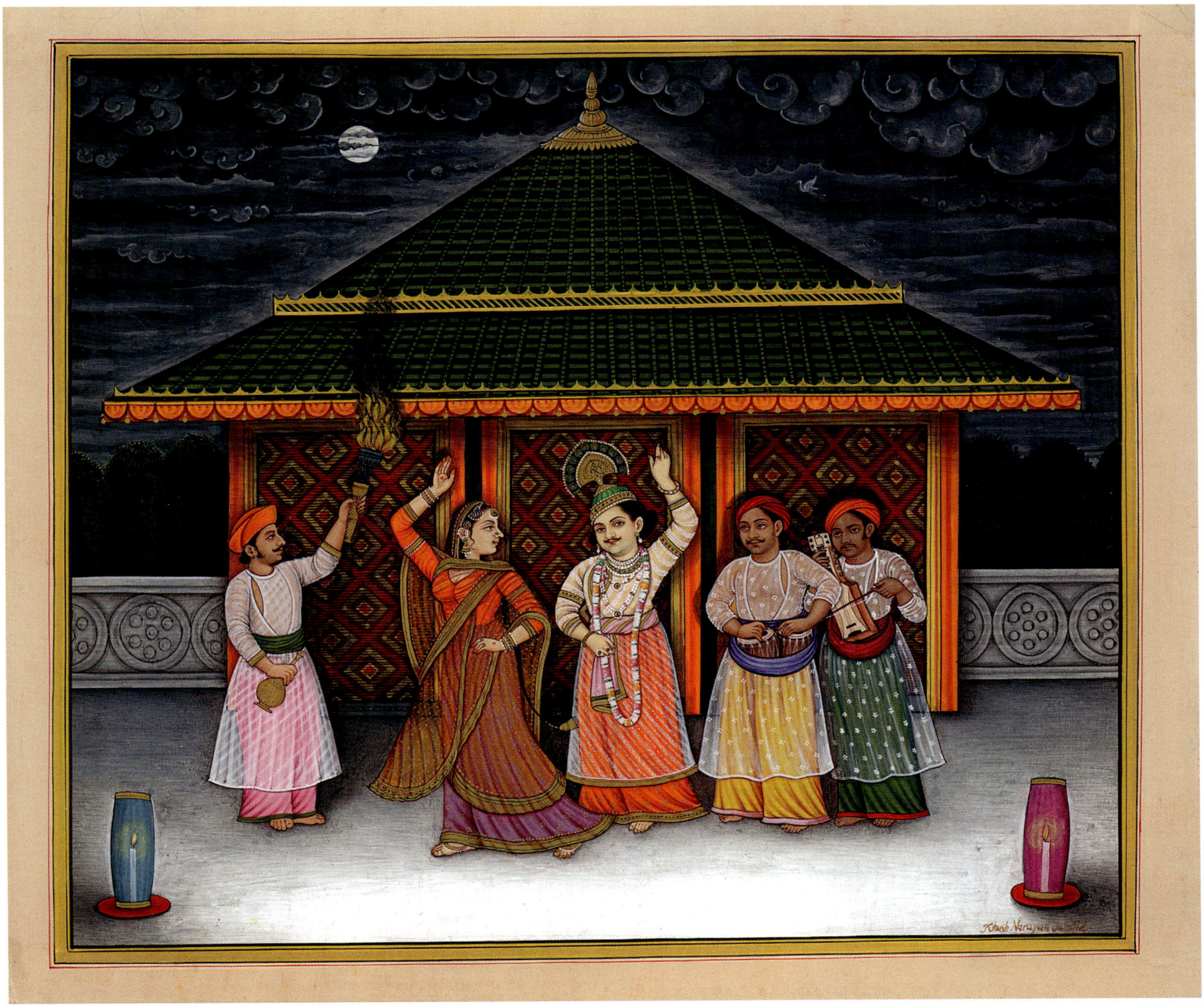

**Artist**: *Khush Narayan Jangid*

# Ganga-Jamuni Tehzeeb

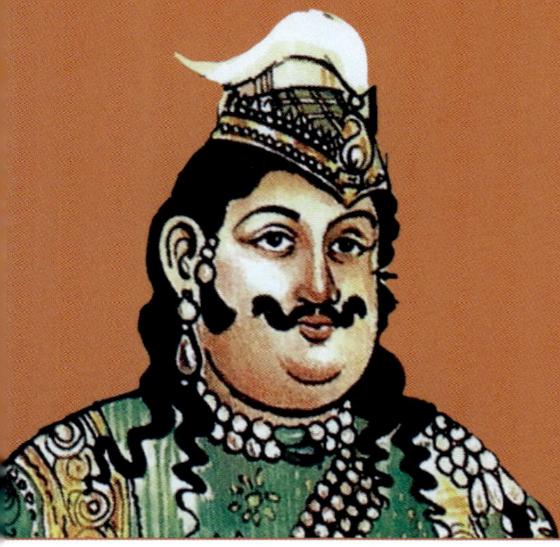

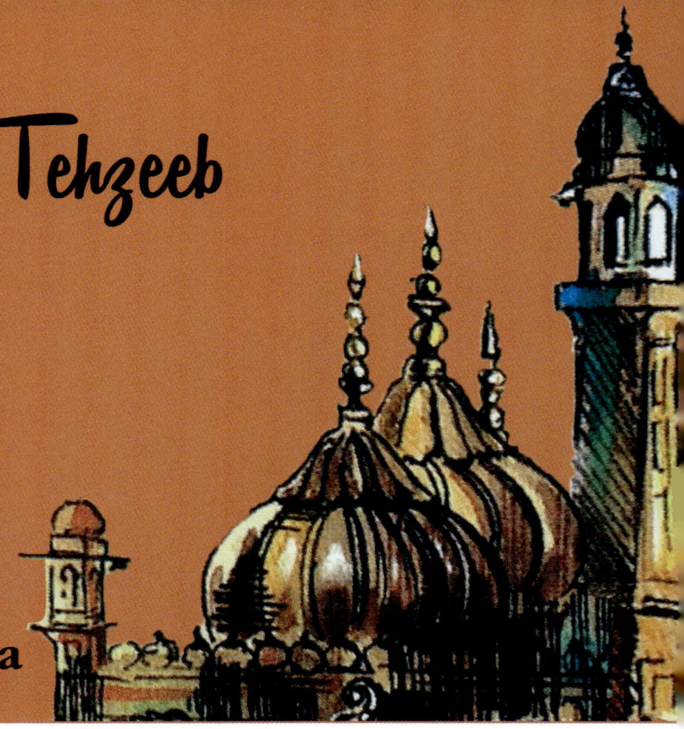

**Nawab Asif Ali Mirza**

There existed a Hindu culture on the banks of the River Jamuna which has been widely spoken and written about. When the Muslim Arabs and Persians settled on the banks of River Ganga, these two cultures started interacting with each other in Doaab – the tongue of land lying between two rivers, in this case, Ganga and Jamuna.

Early on, the Hindus spoke primarily in Hindustani, while the Muslims conversed in Arabic and Persian. As time passed, people started using Persian words while speaking in the Hindustani language. This change, which was caused by the fact that Persian was the official language of the Mughal court, gave birth to a new language. This language was initially called Bhat Khandi (a mixture of Rice and Khand) or the sweet language of Bharat. Later it was named Lashkari, which further came to be known as Urdu.

This interaction between the Hindus and Muslims did not just influence the language but was also responsible for the development of a culture that went on to be known as Ganga–Jamuni Tehzeeb.

When Nawab Sadat Khan Burhan ul Mulk was the Subedar of Awadh, his grandson, Shuja-ud-Daulah, fell ill and was advised to take blessings from Baba Abhay Ram Das. The saint was called upon regularly to bless him. On recovery, Shuja-ud-Daulah gifted a large piece of land to Baba and had a fortress-like walled temple built for him in Hanuman Garhi, Ayodhya. After that, numerous donations were given for the temple.

In turn, Baba Abhay Ram Das built a Mosque on the same land that was gifted to him and arranged Iftar for the Muslims during the holy month of Ramadan. These gestures show how much people respected each other's religion and religious practices, and how it became a part of their *tehzeeb*.

It is pertinent to mention that Shuja-ud-Daulah's son, Asaf-ud-Daulah, walked in the footsteps of his father by gifting a piece of land in Gorakhpur to the Gorakhnath Math. The Gorakhnath Temple was built on the gifted property for the priests of the Math.

This cultural exchange reached its epitome during the rule of Nawab Wajid Ali Shah for which the seeds were sown much earlier. After his birth, astrologers were asked to prepare his astrological chart. They calculated and informed Malka Kishwar that the child was born under the *yog* of Shri Krishna's birth timing; therefore, he would not ascend the throne and be a philosopher instead. Upon hearing this, she was worried and inquired about the ways to overcome this omen. After which she was told that the only way was to offer *puja*s every year on the occasion of Janmashtami and give alms to the poor.

This practice began in secrecy, but after the demise of Amjad Ali Shah, when Wajid Ali Shah ascended the throne, he turned it into a public spectacle. He would take *jog* in a tent for seven days, and on the eighth day, he would appear dressed and posing as Krishna, holding a flute to his lips, while the *gopi*s danced around him. People from Lucknow and surrounding cities would participate in this event, known as Jogi Mela, organized by the *nawab*. The gates of Qaisar Bagh Palace were closed, and only the people who adorned saffron dresses, like the *jogi*s and *jogan*s, were allowed to enter and participate in the *mela*.

He left no stone unturned to ensure that people of all religions, colours, and races felt accommodated in his state. In the Jogi Mela the *nawab* would enact the *Ramayana* and the *Mahabharata*, as prose poems. The last *nawab* of Awadh also had Lanka Kothi built with a folly bridge over which the Vanar Sena would cross to save Sita while enacting *Ramayana*.

Thus, the citizens got involved; the Hindu *pundit*s of Kashmir, who had settled in Kashmir Mohalla of Lucknow, wrote *marsiya*s and *qasida*s (praises of

Prophet Muhammad and family) and participated in reciting them at *majlis* and *mehfil*. Hence respect for each other's religion and culture became an even stronger practice of the time.

Every year on Holi Nawab Wajid Ali Shah made it a custom to play Holi with the people of Lucknow. Once it so happened that the festival of colours coincided with the day of Ashura (the day of martyrdom of Imam Hussain). He was informed that the people of Lucknow were not playing Holi because their *nawab* was observing sorrow over the martyrdom of Imam Hussain. Upon getting this news, he ordered his ministers to let the people know that he would be with them after Asr (approximately 4:30 p.m.) to meet and greet them. After breaking his fast *nawab* went on to meet his people and wish them Holi. What was seen next could be considered the peak of cultural respect, the Hindus, instead of playing with colours, which was a sign of happiness, opted to sprinkle *gulab jal* (rosewater) on the *nawab* and that is how they played Holi!

So this is how the fabric of two distinct cultures, Ganga and Jamuna, was tightly knit to create the silk-like Ganga–Jamuni Tehzeeb.

The Britishers, who at the time were posted in Lucknow, were deeply influenced by the sweet language and culture of the people around them. These blue-eyed foreigners did not just learn the language and adopt the lifestyle, but they also participated in *mushairas* and *mehfils*. Some of them resigned from their services and joined the court of King Wajid Ali Shah. Major Bird was one such example.

The British, who had joined the King of Awadh's service, praised the Lakhnavi culture and recited *ghazals* written by the deposed *nawab*. This act of her people influenced the queen, and she started taking lessons in the Ganga–Jamuni language, i.e. Urdu and culture from a servant, Abdul Karim, who was gifted to her.

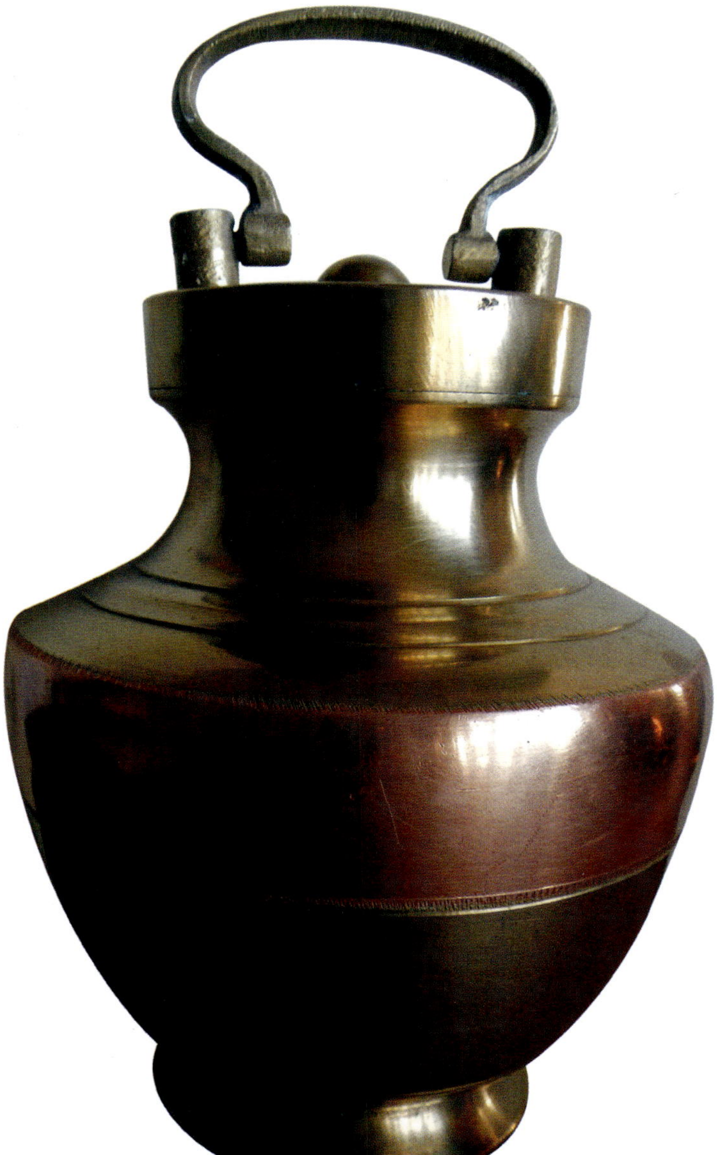

*Ganga Jamuna Lota*

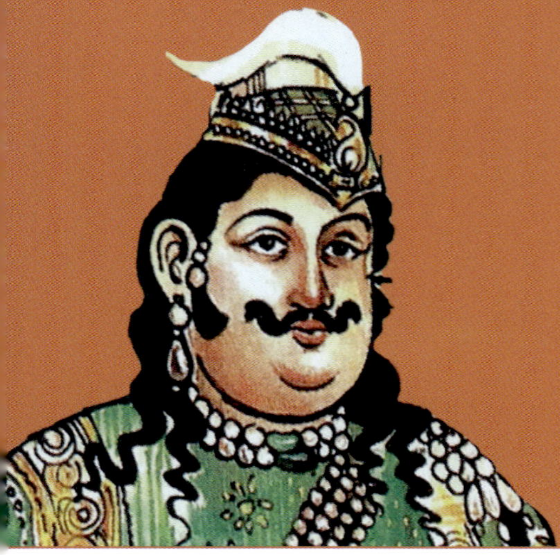

# Authors

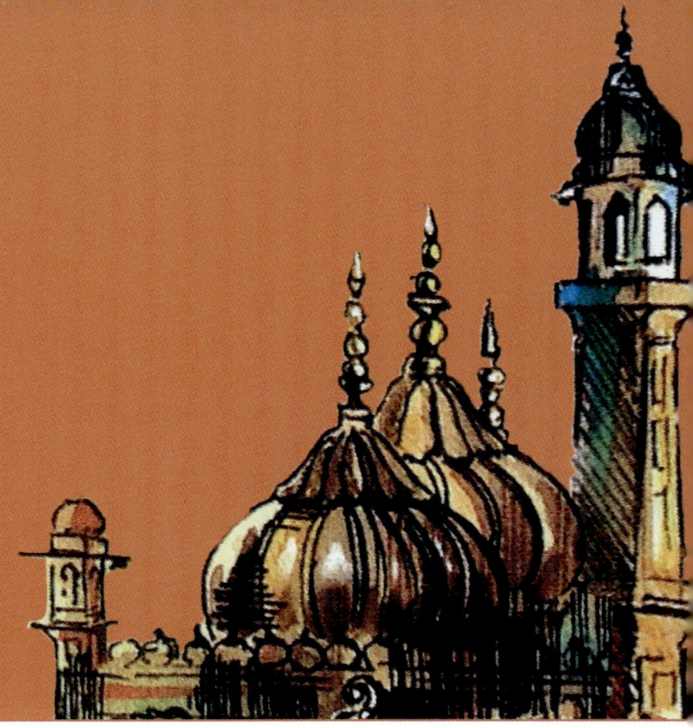

**Muzaffar Ali**

Muzaffar Ali is a painter and filmmaker with a discerning eye and a vision for aesthetics and humanity. He is instrumental in spearheading a movement in upgrading the arts, crafts and culture of the fable city of Lucknow. Muzaffar Ali also entered the field of television serials, documentaries and short films, mainly centred on Awadh, craft, culture, exploitation of women and Sufism. Together with his architect wife Meera Ali, they established Kotwara their international couture brand. He was awarded Yash Bharti Award in 1994, Padma Shri in 2005 and the Rajiv Gandhi Rashtriya Sadbhavana Award in 2014. In 2004, Muzaffar Ali instituted the Rumi Foundation, which holds several Sufi festivals including the World Sufi Music Festival.

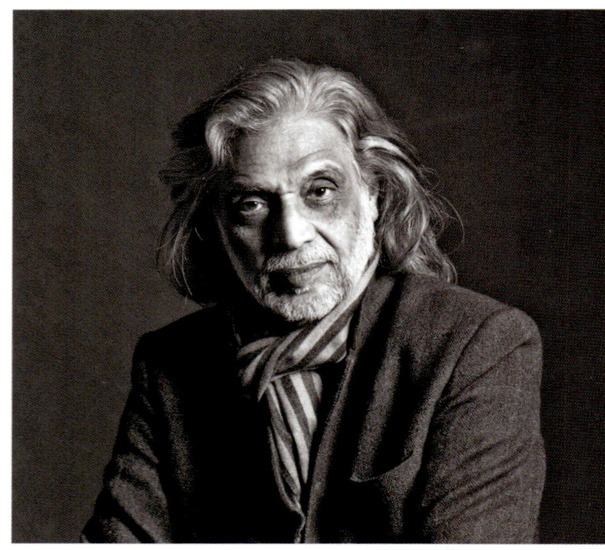

**Harsha V. Dehejia**

Harsha V. Dehejia has a double doctorate, one in Medicine and the other in Ancient Indian Culture, both from Mumbai University. He is also a Member of the Royal College of Physicians of London and a Fellow of the Royal College of Physicians of Canada, both by examination. He is a practising Physician and Professor of Indic Studies in the College of the Humanities of Carleton University in Ottawa, Canada. He has more than 25 books to his credit, 4 short films and many curated exhibitions.

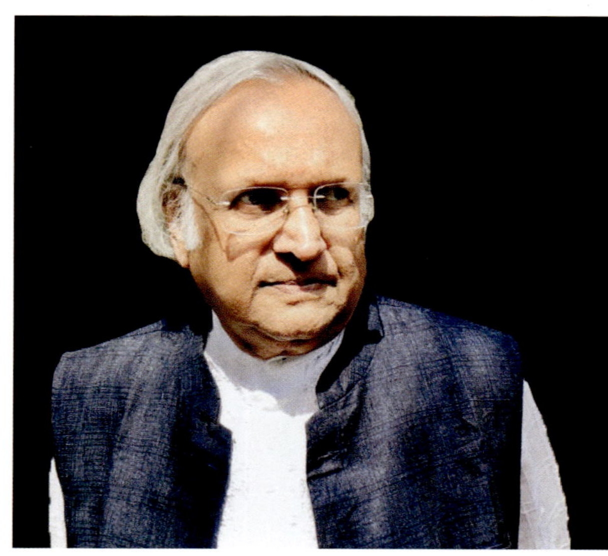

**Dr Shovana Narayan**

Guru Dr Shovana Narayan has relentlessly pursued two parallel exacting professional careers, achieving distinction and great heights in both. She is a well-known and venerated Kathak guru–performer–choreographer and has also served in the civil services, Indian Audit and Accounts till her retirement. She has an MSc in Physics, 2 MPhil degrees and a Doctor of Letters (HC). She has authored over 16 books, presented several research papers and contributed well over 200 articles. Shovana has been decorated by the Government of India with the Padma Shri award in 1992 and the Sangeet Natak Akademi award in 2001, besides being a recipient of over 35 national and international awards.

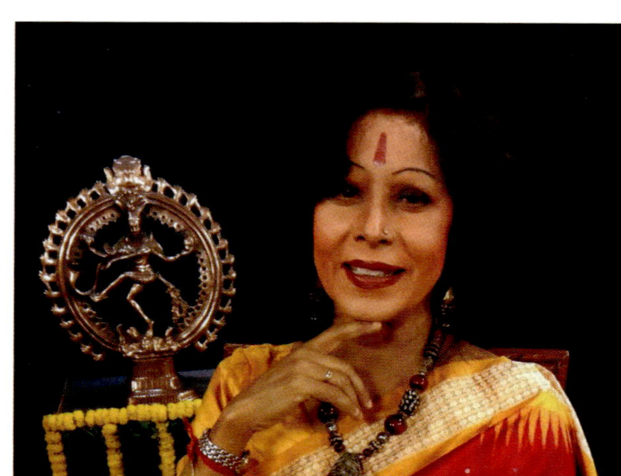

**Dr Richard David Williams**

Dr Richard David Williams is Lecturer in Ethnomusicology at SOAS University of London. He was previously a Leverhulme Early Career Fellowship at the University of Oxford (2015-17). A cultural historian of music, his research brings music and sound studies into conversation with the study of religion and Indian cultural history. He is currently finalizing his first monograph, on the circulation of musicians, genres and musicologists between upper India and Bengal between *c.*1750–1900. In connection to this project, he has written on Bengali-language musicology, the performance repertoires of courtesans and sound arts in Shi'ah Islam. His wider work has explored musical culture in seventeenth- and eighteenth-century South Asia. His research languages are Hindi, Brajbhasha, Bengali, Urdu and Maithili.

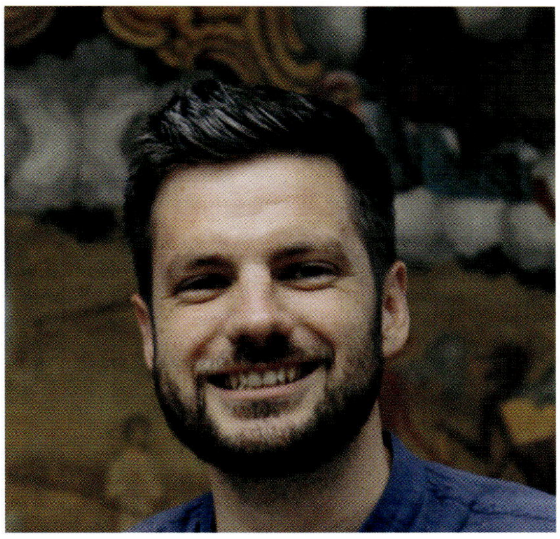

**Sunil Sunkara**

Sunil Sunkara identifies himself as a new-age Indian with a modern outlook yet traditional approach to life. He is a recipient of the President's National Balashri Honour in the field of Innovative Science and the Multicultural Leadership Award from the University of Wisconsin-Madison, USA. He started training in Kathak in 2006 under the guidance of Natalia Hildner and Kiran Chouhan in the US. Since 2009 he has been learning Kathak under the guidance of Renu Sharma at Kalashram Mumbai, under the aegis of Padmavibhushan Pt Birju Maharaj. Sunil did his Nritya Nipun in Kathak securing a first division from the Bhatkhande Sangit Vidyapith, Lucknow. He has done his Masters in Kathak securing a gold medal from Kavikulaguru Kalidas Sanskrit University, Ramtek. He has done a Diploma in "Natyashatra with Reference to Kathak" from Bharata College of Fine Arts & Culture, Mumbai, where he is also currently the faculty for Dance Theory.

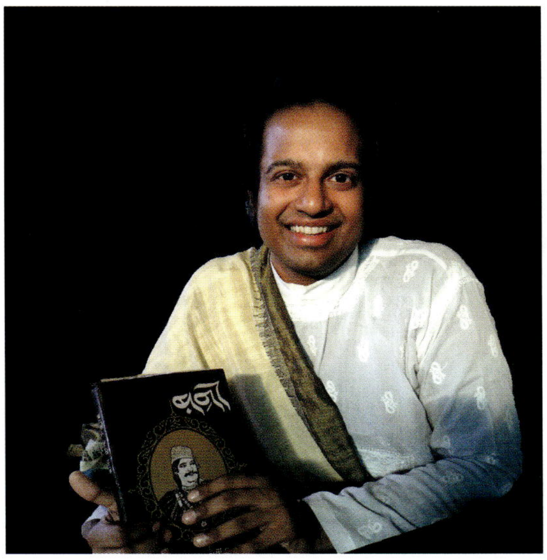

**Malini Roy**

Malini Roy is the Head of Visual Arts at the British Library, London. She received her PhD in art history from the School of Oriental and African Studies at the University of London; her doctoral thesis focused on the idiosyncrasies in the late Mughal painting tradition and concentrated on the artist Mihr Chand (fl. *c.*1759-86). In 2012, she curated the Library's exhibition Mughal India: Art, Culture and Empire and co-authored the accompanying publication with J.P. Losty. In 2008, she curated and authored, 50 x India: The 50 Most Beautiful Miniatures from the Rijksmuseum.

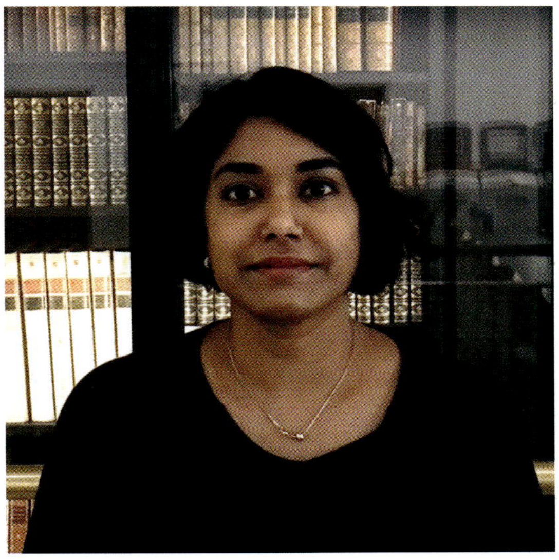

**Nawab Asif Ali Mirza**

Nawab Asif Ali Mirza is the direct descendant of Nawab Wajid Ali Shah of both the maternal and paternal sides and is a living exponent of Wajid Ali Shah's artistic oeuvre.

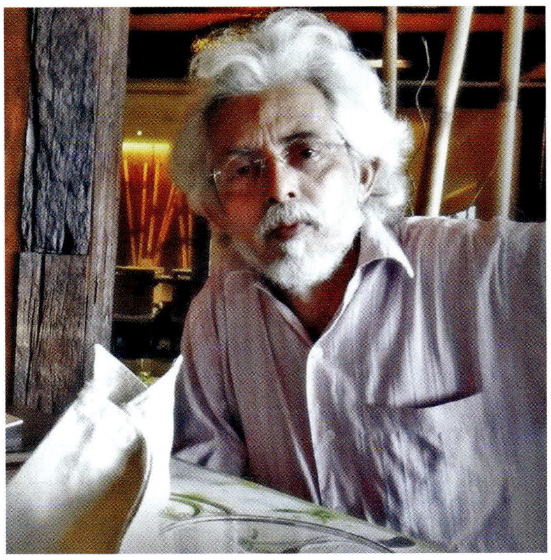

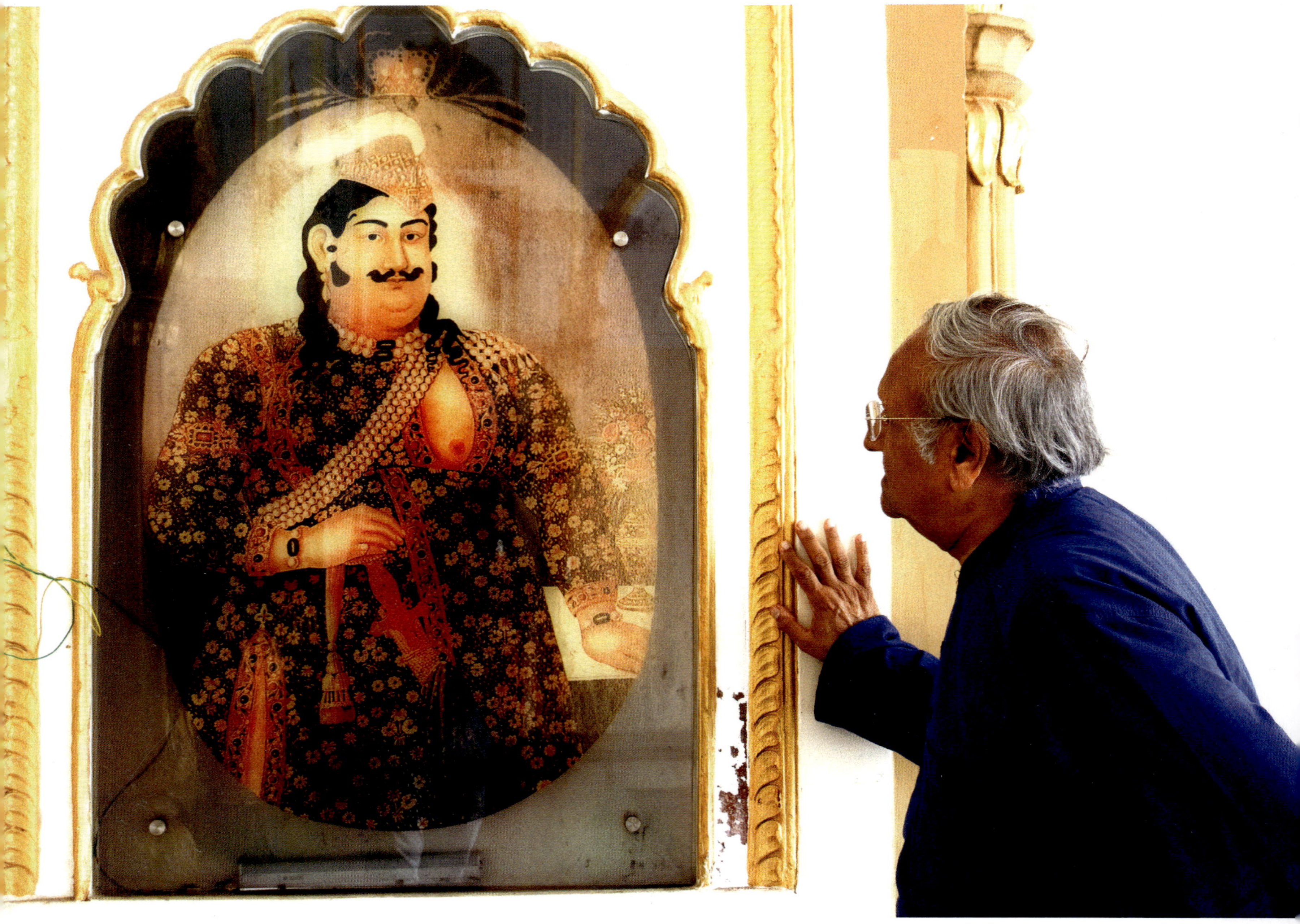